Organized Simplicity

The Clutter-Free Approach to Intentional Living

by Tsh Oxenreider

BETTERWAY HOME
CINCINNATI, OHIO
WWW.BETTERWAYBOOKS.COM

Other fine Betterway Home Books are available from your local bookstore, or online, or direct from the publisher. Visit our website, www.fwmedia.com.

14   13   12   11   5   4   3   2

Distributed in Canada by Fraser Direct
100 Armstrong Avenue, Georgetown, Ontario, Canada L7G 5S4, Tel: (905) 877-4411
Distributed in the U.K. and Europe by F+W Media International
Brunel House, Newton Abbot, Devon, TQ12 4PU, England, Tel: (+44) 1626 323200,
Fax: (+44) 1626 323319, E-mail: postmaster@davidandcharles.co.uk
Distributed in Australia by Capricorn Link
P.O. Box 704, S. Windsor NSW, 2756 Australia, Tel: (02) 4577-3555

Library of Congress Cataloging in Publication Data
Oxenreider, Tsh
  Organized simplicity : a clutter-free approach to intentional living / by Tsh Oxenreider. -- 1st ed.
       p. cm.
  Includes index.
  ISBN 978-1-4403-0263-3 (hardcover : alk. paper)
  1. House cleaning. 2. Storage in the home. 3. Time management. I. Title.
  TX324.O79 2010
  648'.8--dc22
                                      2010019266

Edited by Jacqueline Musser; designed by Clare Finney; production coordinated by Mark Griffin. Photos on pages 36 and 186 by Tsh Oxenreider. Photos on pages 12–13, 96 and 118 by Angie Warren. Photos on pages 166 and 167 by Rachel Meeks.

About the Author

Tsh Oxenreider is the creator of the
popular blog SimpleMom.net and is the
founder of SimpleLivingMedia.com.
She is passionate about simplifying life
and eliminating clutter so that the truly
meaningful things in life can breathe.
Tsh spends her days with her husband
and three young children—exploring the
world, reading and learning, and being
inspired by whatever surroundings their
travels take them to. To learn more about
her projects, visit TshOxenreider.com.

Dedication

To Kyle—I wouldn't want to live life with anyone else.

Acknowledgments

Thank you to F+W Media for taking a chance on a first-time blogger-turned-author, and to my editor, Jackie Musser, for your ongoing support and encouragement.

Thanks, also, to the many fabulous people I've been blessed to know online and who contributed in some way to the crafting of this book (even indirectly, just through their encouragement): Corey Allan, Maya Bissineer, Lisa Byrne, Mandi Ehman, Kara Fleck, Katie Fox, Barbara Jones, Marie LeBaron, Lisa Leonard, Shannon Lowe, Jamie Martin, Rachel Meeks, Melissa Michaels, Nester, Crystal Paine, Charlie and Sarah Park, Meredith Pelham, Heidi Scovel, Amanda Soule, Megan Tietz, Ann Voskamp, Emily Walker, Aimée Wimbush-Bourque, Alli Worthington, and the many others with whom I am honored to share the blogosphere. I am better because of you all.

Thank you to Cheryl Carrell, Ali Glass, Lisa Henke, Kerin Hurley, Natasha Kohlmann, Heather Lewis, Melanie Lloyd, Rachel McAdams, Meena Matocha, Kristi Naizer, Clarisa Rhodes, Amy Scott, Ginny Tittel, Lisa Van Allen, and Brooke Wagen for your ongoing friendship. If I had it my way, I'd put you all in one room and give you a giant group hug. I suppose that will have to wait until Heaven.

Thank you to Hannah Wheeler, who watched my little ones so that I could scribble away on this book. My kids love you, and because of you, this book actually happened.

Thank you to all the readers of SimpleMom.net, for providing me with a writing platform miraculously equipped with speakers. I am honored and humbled beyond measure that you would spend some of your day with me. I am so grateful for you.

Thank you to my family—to Mom and Dad, to Josh, Joan, Nellie, Holden, Ed, Linda, Darren, Carly, Aaron, Ashton, and Carsyn. I am blessed beyond belief to have a family as supportive as you all are. Thanks for your encouragement, for your interest in my work, and for your inspiration. And thanks for loving me as I am.

To Tate and Reed, my little darlings who make me laugh, cry, and stand before God in awe: Thank you for the awesome privilege of being your mama. It is truly the best job on Earth. And to the little guy kicking inside me as I type—I can't wait to meet you. You are forever welcome in this family.

Finally, to my biggest cheerleader, chef, chauffer, admin, comrade, friend, confidante, and life mate: Kyle, I still can't believe how blessed I am to be married to you. Thank you for your nonstop support as I wrote this book and put other things to the side for a season. You are a gift, and I love you.

Contents

Introduction

Simple living is not easy, ironically. It's hard to know where to start, what steps to take, and what it really looks like. Most simple living books are inundated with theories, step-by-step plans, and experts who can tell you *exactly* what your simple life should look like.

This is not one of those books. Sure, there are checklists and tasks to help you on your journey toward a simpler life. But at the foundation of this book is the idea of *redefining simplicity*. You must understand simple living as something more than just a catch phrase, some pie-in-the-sky ambition, a trend. Only *then* will you find the motivation to create a simpler life that works for you, your family, and your home. I want to help you find what simple living looks like for *you*.

Personally, I've always craved a simple life. As our culture progresses toward *more* busyness, *more* options, and *more* opportunities to make money, my heart runs the other way. Sure, I value working from home (I am a blogger and entrepreneur, after all). And I'm thankful for the choices of cereals down the grocery store aisle most of the time. But adding more choices often only adds *more* stress to our lives. One hundred years ago, a housewife didn't have an endless selection of toothpastes. She probably had one option she could buy at her local apothecary, or she could make her own. And she didn't complain about her lack of toothpaste choices or flavors—she didn't know any different because that's just the way life was back then.

Are we any happier today because we can choose from twenty different toothpaste brands and thirty different flavors between them all? Maybe our teeth are a bit healthier, but we're not any more content as a culture. We're stressed.

Occam's razor states that when you have two competing theories that make exactly the same predictions, the simpler one is the better. In parenting, I apply this to mean *keep it simple*. Don't buy a baby wipes warmer—hold the wipe in your hand for a few seconds to warm it up. Don't create some complicated chore system that neither you nor your children can understand—simply give them assignments and privileges for accomplishing them. You don't need an expensive system that helps you teach your children to read—read to them all the time, and teach them phonics. All things being equal, always choose the simpler option. It'll save your sanity.

This theory rings true in home and family management as well. There is no reason to complicate your family culture just because the culture at large is complicated. When you choose the simple road over the one cluttered with gadgets, theories, and systems, your whole family will probably have more peace and less stress.

And at the end of the day, that's what truly matters—a family and a home at peace. A home full of people, content with their belongings, their relationships, and their available time.

This doesn't happen passively or quickly—there are proactive, sometimes difficult steps you have to embrace and tackle with gusto. *Organized Simplicity's* goal is to outline this process in a clear-cut, methodical, and sanity-saving process. To make it even clearer, here is what you can expect to accomplish as you work through this book:

- ☐ Memorize the definition of simple living: "Living holistically with your life's purpose" (chapter 2)
- ☐ Create your family's purpose statement (chapter 3)
- ☐ Evaluate your family's current commitments and schedule (chapter 4)
- ☐ Start a routine of evaluating your family's weekly appointments with your spouse (chapter 4)

- [ ] Make a plan to get out of debt (chapter 5)
- [ ] Make a plan to save six months' of expenses for an emergency fund (chapter 5)
- [ ] Make a plan to start saving for retirement and your kids' higher education (chapter 5)
- [ ] Write down words you'd like to describe your home's overall atmosphere (chapter 8)
- [ ] Label each room in your home with its purpose (chapter 8)
- [ ] Put a yard sale on the calendar for sometime in the next two months (chapter 9)
- [ ] Declutter, clean, and organize the:
    - Living room
    - Kitchen
    - Bathrooms
    - Kids' rooms
    - Master bedroom
    - Front entry, coat closet, and back patio or balcony

My deepest wish is that this book changes your perspective on life at home. It's written as a jump start to get you started on a newfound road toward a simpler life, one many home managers have traveled in previous generations. I'd love for you to join me on this journey. Let's revive the beauty of simple living. It's well worth the effort.

PART ONE

Living Simply in the Real World

1 | Stuff

Our Modern-Day Slave Master

"Too many people spend money
they haven't earned, to buy
things they don't want, to
impress people they don't like."

–WILL ROGERS

What does it look like for a modern-day family to live simply while still participating in afterschool sports, errand running, and getting enough sleep to not go insane? Simple living is about living your life with a purpose that aligns with your values. It's about enjoying the things you love and care about and not about stressing over the things that don't matter. It's fulfilling; it brings peace; it drips with contentment. Living simply is about being who you were made to be.

That's what this book is about. I want to park at the nitty-gritty of life—the intersection between good intentions and reality. I want to help you find that peaceful place, where your pocketbook, your home, and your weekly routine reflect your family's convictions and values.

Responsible home managers must be intentional with their decisions—we need to take time to evaluate our priorities and then take the steps necessary to make our family life reflect the simple life we crave. It won't happen *for* us—mature adults proactively make decisions and form habits to shape their home lives into the lifestyles they desire. We can't blame a hectic schedule, too many bills to pay, or too many messes to clean for keeping us from our goals because we can do something about those. You want a simpler life at home for your family—a home that is clean and organized and fits your life's purpose. I want to give you some tools to help you do this.

Admitting that I'm not a certified organizer or a simplicity guru is probably not the best way to begin a book about simple living. But I need to lay that out on the table between me and you, the reader, before we begin this journey together. I don't have a database full of clients, and I don't have my own TV show. I'm a young mom running a busy household. Maybe you can relate. Simple living is something I've learned to value through my life experience. It's been a long journey to get here, and it's a journey you can take as well. In fact, I'm still walking the path.

My husband and I have made simplicity one of our lives' highest priorities. We currently live outside of the United States in a 1,400-square-foot apartment (boasting only one closet) with our five-year-old daughter, our two-year-old son, and another little one on the way. We continually evaluate all of our belongings to make sure they still offer value to our lives. We are selective with the new purchases we bring in our home in order to make the most of our space. We hardly watch any television, and we spend lots of time together because both my husband and I work from home. These intentional decisions allow us to live a life that feels right in a way that corresponds with our highest values. We're able to live on a rather meager salary while still enjoying family outings, the occasional vacation, and even quality coffee. But our lifestyle didn't happen overnight. My life's journey has helped shape my philosophy about simple living.

Craving Intentionality

I grew up in a very normal American environment, ripe in the suburbs of Austin, Texas, in the 1980s, with my parents and my brother, who is five years my junior. Both my parents worked outside the home, and I spent my afterschool hours watching TV, playing with neighborhood kids, and going to ballet class. I attended public school and was a good student. My family was well rooted, and we lived in the same house for sixteen of my first eighteen years of life. My childhood was happy. You could say we were a typical family living an average upper-middle-class life.

At age eighteen, I moved out and cut the apron strings. My life up to that point seemed complete, but I had a nagging sense of being a bit unprepared for real life—the nuts and bolts that actually make life work.

While I was single and in my mid-twenties, I traveled internationally and saw the way many other cultures lived. I was inspired by what I experienced, but I still didn't know what I was made for. I knew I wanted to run a home that was full of kids, a husband, and love. But I felt like I didn't know how to manage a home, a most basic life skill. My problem was, I didn't quite know *what* that house full of love and family should look like. I enjoyed my childhood, so it wasn't as if I wanted a 180 for my own kids. But I wanted more ... intentionality in my life. More conviction. More certainty about the *why* behind the decisions I made as a home manager. I didn't want life to happen to me; I wanted to happen to life.

Moving Abroad

My husband and I married with the intention of one day moving overseas. We didn't know any specifics, but we knew that if our plan were to become a reality, we'd have to not bury our roots too deeply, too soon. So from the beginning of our marriage, we made it a priority not to collect too much stuff. This would make moving abroad easier.

Good intentions didn't keep life from happening. Even though our wedding registry was fairly Spartan, we still managed to need more storage space than our 1,000-square-foot apartment gave us. Our daughter, Tatum, was born just after our two-year anniversary, and with her came the toys typical of a firstborn child. It wasn't bad, mind you, but we knew it wasn't what we intended.

Our goal of moving abroad remained a priority, but we still accumulated almost $20,000 in debt (most of it being my student loans from college). My husband worked as many hours as possible while I stayed home with Tate so that our dream of living abroad could happen within the first decade of our marriage, not during our empty-nest years.

When we paid off all but the school loans, we were more or less ready to make the big move. But before we could leave, we had all of our belongings to contend with. It wasn't sane to trek 6,000 miles across the ocean with a full household, so a massive purge was in order. This purge took time, energy, and a few tears. We questioned every one of our possessions. I knew that we could buy bedding, furniture, and home décor in other countries, but it was still difficult to know what to part with and what was worth our precious luggage space.

I handed to the God of all good things my desire to create an ideal nest for my family, and we sold most of our stuff. The kitchen gadgets, the curtains, the artwork in my daughter's room—all were sold in a massive garage sale.

We packed everything we had decided to keep into fifteen boxes, which became our check-in luggage for a twenty-three-hour flight. These were all of our earthly possessions for a family of three (minus a few quilts and yearbooks, which we kept in storage in the States). And surprisingly, I was at peace about it. I brought with us a few cooking utensils (ones I wasn't sure I could find in our new country), my favorite books, some movies, and our best-fitting clothes. We left behind our rather new dishes, towels, and bedding, along with any books, movies, or clothes we no longer loved. I trusted that we could find decent replacements in our new home and that many of the things I thought were essential really weren't. I still kept the things that would be hard to replace (books in English, for example), and of course, I never parted with our family photos.

Letting Go

Before we moved abroad, I wouldn't have believed you if you had told me I would be fine not having my pewter fruit bowl, the flea-market coffee table I personally refurbished, or the buffet my husband crafted with his own two hands. I've never been a hoarder, but I love nesting. My home is my haven, and I've wanted to create my own since I was a little girl. The way some people love shoes, or perhaps a few of you drool over the latest gadgets, is the way I am about the ideal armchair for our master bedroom, or the perfect summer scent from a soy candle in the kitchen. I *love* nesting.

But I've come to realize that those things are just *things*, and that while they aren't inherently evil, they can actually erode my family's purpose in life—or at least water down the potency of our choices. They can multiply the surfaces I need to dust. They can dwindle my checking account. They can even cause stress. And they can keep my family from living life to the fullest because we've slowly allowed our stuff to own us. Our purpose in life is directly related to how we define simple living. So if our possessions chip away at our purpose, so, too, goes a simpler life, no matter how noble our intentions.

You may be thinking I'm extreme, and you just can't or don't want to live life the way I do. That's okay. We all have different goals and values. Your vision of a simple life will not be the same as mine. But I want to encourage you to carefully evaluate the things you allow into your home and life. Are they truly making you happy? According to the statistics, they probably are not.

The Inflated Floor Plan

National Public Radio reports that from 1950 to 2004, the average American home has doubled in size—what was once 983 square feet is now 2,349 square feet.[1] That's a 1,366-square-foot addition—an entire second house.

According to the U.S. Census Bureau, the average family in 1950 consisted of 3.67 members.[2] In 2002, the average family size was 2.62 members. Today, smaller families "need" bigger homes, and the trend doesn't stop in America. Australia, New Zealand, and most of the Westernized world are all seeing the same trend. The average home size in Australia is 2,200 square feet; in New Zealand it's 1,900.[3]

Do we really think we need almost 900 square feet per person in our homes today? That's what the numbers indicate if we do simple math. Today we live in homes that provide almost the same amount of room *per person* that an average 1950s-size house would have provided for an *entire family* (when the average family size was larger than it is today).

Average Square Footage of a New Single-Family Home

1950	983
1970	1,500
1990	2,080
2004	2,349

Source: National Association of Home Builders (Housing Facts, Figures and Trends for March 2006)

Overworked and Overbooked

It's not just floor plans that have inflated; the average workload has increased as well. By law, Australians receive four weeks of paid vacation; Europeans usually receive four to five weeks. There are no vacation laws in the United States to guarantee its citizens any time off of work. One in four working Americans don't receive any paid vacation at all. Those who do average only fifteen days annually.[4] We are quickly becoming the most overworked culture in the history of the world.

Being overworked isn't reserved for working adults. After my first child was born, I noticed a sense of urgency had trickled into the veins of children. I watched with astonishment at how busy kids were becoming. Eight-year-olds were taxied across town for cello lessons, pottery class, and extracurricular Italian lessons, all in the name of well-roundedness. Fewer and fewer children ran around the neighborhood, and goofing around at the local pool was replaced with supervised play dates. I held my infant baby and wondered if the same fate was inevitable for me and for her.

Five years later, that infant girl has a toddler brother, and I don't see much around me changing. Frugality is trendier, but life's craziness hasn't slowed. Families have declared it more and more impossible to live on one income. Mamas who want to stay at home with their young kids can't crunch the numbers to make it happen, so they have succumbed to the 8-to-5 business day, dressing in suits and playing roles they don't really want. It is for their kids, so that Ethan and Ashley can attend all those extracurricular activities—but no one is really happy about the whole setup.

What's the Deal?

These inflated homes and out-of-control work expectations don't make us happy. According to a study done by Italy's Siena University in 2007, the average American paycheck has risen over the past thirty years (even when adjusted for inflation), but a drop in the quality of the workers' personal relationships offsets the emotional benefits of the increased salary.[5] We have more money but fewer meaningful relationships, and less time to enjoy the ones we do have. We work, and work, and then work some more, yet have little more than "stuff" to show for it.

With more space to clutter, less time for relationships, and almost no freedom for a vacation from work, we are stressed. We're on a hamster wheel running to keep up with life. Instead of getting off the wheel, we're frantically searching for ways we can increase our endurance and keep up. We buy bigger cars to haul our things and buy fancier phones to keep track of our kids' calendars and family meal plans.

Instead of adjusting to the hamster wheel, how about we find a completely different way to live life?

Simple Living: The Latest Buzzword

Simple living is a buzzword in our postmodern culture, and concepts like frugality and going green are trendy. They offer smart moves toward a healthier planet and healthier families. But the basic problem beneath these trends is that they feel like they ask so much of us. These ideas ask us to move into a world that feels impossible for everyday families who still want to participate in Little League, and who don't really want to live off the grid.

Sell your cars and transport your family around on bikes. It's a great idea if you live in a metropolis with convenient public transportation, or in a tiny town with errands no more than a few miles away. But more than 50 percent of Americans live in the suburbs.[6] I'm not sure too many of those folks are privy to abandoning their motor vehicles. Most of us don't need gas-guzzling SUVs, but it's probably not realistic to expect everyone to completely swear off fossil fuel consumption.

Abandon your big-box grocery store and eat only from your garden. It's a fun idea, and more families are catching on to the urban homesteading movement. But 80 percent of American households are two-income families and many people don't feel like they have the time required to make this option possible.

Wear clothing made from only organic material, woven in a free-trade factory. Indeed, we should all support businesses that take the extra step to ensure a better quality of life for the less fortunate, and that create quality, earth-friendly material. But until prices can be lowered, the average Jane can't spend the money it would cost to clothe her entire family in this garb. She still needs to pay the mortgage.

If we can't do all of these things, where does that leave us? It seems like we need to completely redefine simple living. Let's take some time to define what *realistic* simple living looks like for you. There's no need to forsake the suburbs for the farm.

2 | Simple Living

Discover a Definition that Works for You

"The simplest things are
often the truest."

–RICHARD BACH

At the end of World War II, architects began planning a new hybrid of city and country living that was not quite urban but not quite rural, and thus the name the *suburbs*. With the Industrial Revolution in the pages of history for nearly forty years, most families didn't need to live in cities near factories for work. These young families craved a quieter life with a patch of grass. But they wanted the convenience of city life that farms didn't provide—a place close enough to the city so they could drive their Studebaker in for food, household supplies, and clothes.

Settled just a few miles outside a metropolis, the suburbs provided an ultimate blend of serene living and convenience. And now, in the twenty-first century, suburbs make up a huge portion of the American landscape—more than 50 percent of us live in them. We can't imagine a city without it surrounded by myriad neighborhoods peppered with fences and flowerbeds, elementary schools and soccer fields.

Suburbs are a quintessential part of Westernized life. They provide square footage under a roof, a portion of land for gardens or trampolines, a decent school district (usually), and an easy place to park two cars. They're convenient, and they're where most of our available real estate is found.

It's easy, however, to shelter our families in these suburbs. When all of our friends *also* live in surrounding suburbs with the same layout as our own, it's hard to imagine having anything less than a fifth of an acre for a backyard, a 26-cubic-foot refrigerator, and a fully equipped laundry room with a washer and a dryer. We want these conveniences, and life is hard to imagine without them.

There's no reason to apologize for owning them, so long as we remember that these things are *luxuries*, not necessities. In 2005, more than three billion people (half the world's population) lived on less than $2 (U.S.) a day. Eighty percent of the world lives without running water or electricity. If you live in the United States, you're among the 6 percent of the world's wealthiest people.[7] These numbers aren't meant to give you a guilt trip—they're simply a reality check. The items in our homes that we feel we absolutely "need" are downright extravagances within the global landscape.

So if we keep these luxuries—our ACs, our gargantuan refrigerators, our deep freezers in the garage, and our clothes dryers—what does it really look like to simplify?

Here's What Simple Living Is Not

1. Living on a Homestead, Off the Grid, or Without Electricity or Cars

It's true—there are a few hardy, modern-day homesteaders in the Western world who manage to live without refrigerators, who ride bicycles everywhere (kids included), and who reuse their toilet paper. It's what they want, and best wishes to them.

Most of us can't voluntarily swallow that pill. Our luxuries may not be necessities for survival, but they sure are nice, and in some cases they make simple living easier. A bulk freezer can definitely help some families with their meal planning. A fuel-efficient car makes errand running fast enough to enjoy the rewards of a simple home. And I probably don't need to tell you that electricity makes home life just a *little* easier and more pleasant.

So simplifying your life and home does not mean needing to go to extremes. You can still enjoy modern comforts.

2. More Work

You might think simplifying your home means sacrificing convenience to the point where *more* work is actually created, not less. Sure, cloth diapers are less expensive and better for the environment, but don't they require more maintenance and work? How would they simplify things? Growing a vegetable garden can be a cheap way to fill our bodies with good things, but who has the time to weed and hoe and water and fertilize when there's dry cleaning to pick up?

Simplifying your life is meant to make things better, not worse. It's about choices—about saying *no* to the things in your life that aren't the best so that you are free and available to say *yes* to those things you truly want.

3. Only for the Cuckoos

The phrase "simple living" can sound a bit … out there. Like it's for the granola-types, or the families who live in tiny towns—or even more, it's for the people without kids and real-life commitments. It's easy to hear this phrase and wonder, *Who on earth can live like this?*

When simplicity is married to reality, it *is* possible. Not only is it possible, it's quite possibly the best way to live life. Each family ultimately has its own description of what "simple living" looks like, and each family should strive for a simple life in its own ways. Your children, as well as your stress level and your sanity, will thank you.

Simple living does not require giving up those things you love or swearing off those things that make twenty-first century living possible. It simply requires you to simplify your life. For more on this, see Appendix D for a discussion on current simplicity trends.

So What Is Simple Living?

If what I've described so far is what simple living *isn't*, then just what *is* simple living? Not at all ironically, my definition is simple. It applies to everybody, it's timeless, and it's not bound by cultural trends or norms. It can be your definition for the rest of your life, and it will apply to your life, no matter where you live and regardless of your life stage. The definition of simple living is this: *living holistically with your life's purpose.* That's it.

Let's break this phrase into its parts.

Living Holistically

"Holistic" means to emphasize the importance of the whole and the interdependence of its parts. All the parts work together for the good of the whole, and the final result—the whole—matters more than any single, independent part. Much like a delectable chocolate chip cookie requires brown sugar, eggs, flour, and chocolate chips, so, too, does simple living require individual ingredients combined into one final product. Chocolate chips and brown sugar are good by themselves, but they're much better mixed and baked together into a mouth-watering cookie.

Holistic living means that your spiritual, relational, emotional, intellectual, physical, and financial lives are working together. They're not competing with one another. One area doesn't scream out for attention to the detriment of another area of your life; these parts exist to complement and strengthen one another. And pointed in the same direction, each of these parts causes your life—the whole—to flow seamlessly and peacefully. Each part's focus is the same—to play a role in completing the whole.

With Your Life's Purpose

Your life's purpose may look different than your neighbor's purpose depending on your priorities, your worldview, and your value system. But ultimately, we all have a purpose. Your purpose is the reason for which you exist, for which you do things, and for which you are made. It is what you are *about*. It's the reason you live.

So if you have a family, the members of your family have a collective purpose—to function as a family unit. Ideally, each family member will work for the good of the other members so that the entire family unit functions holistically. Each member's function will be different, but the functions should all benefit the family as a whole. There is a reason you are the family that you are, and you are unique from other families.

So when you apply this new definition of simple living to your life, the different parts of your life line up in the same direction, and that direction is pointed toward your life's purpose. All the independent things in your life— the items you own, how you spend your time, the relationships you cultivate, and the books you read—ultimately benefit your life's purpose. There is no clutter. Your hours and days and weeks reflect your priorities, and so does the space in which you live. As a family, you're united for something bigger than each of you separately, and you all are parts that complete the holistic family unit. We'll discuss how to discover your life's purpose in chapter 3.

Four Extra Benefits of Simplifying and Decluttering

So in addition to living out your life's purpose, there are at least four extra advantages to simplifying and decluttering your home and life, and each of these contributes to the overall goal of living holistically with your life's purpose. No one should miss out on these treasures.

When we get rid of stuff in our homes and declutter, there are the obvious benefits of freed-up square footage and fewer surfaces to clean. But let's not forget some additional side effects we'll experience by tossing needless stuff in our lives.

1. More Time for People

When we have more stuff, we usually have less time for relationships with other people. How many times have you wanted to invite another family over for dinner and games, but didn't because of Mt. Laundry on the couch and the food scraps stuck to the kitchen counters? Or did your son recently want to invite a playmate over for an afternoon of Lego building, but instead he needed to suit up for ball practice in between piano lessons and his sister's ballet class?

Our homes and our calendars are filled to the brim, and someone has to take care of those things. Responsible adults do their best to keep their homes sanitary and to honor their commitments. But it's a bummer when being responsible means being chained to your stuff and your schedules, instead of enjoying relationships in a slower-paced way.

There's a hidden opportunity cost to owning materials things. If we choose a complete set of everyday dishes, formal china, a single-use appliance for every cooking task, and state-of-the-art cookware that requires maintenance and care, we'll probably need a kitchen big enough to fit it all. And a bigger kitchen takes longer to clean than a smaller one. It might seem like small potatoes, but when your home takes longer to clean, it means more time each day or week devoted to the task. The hidden opportunity cost? More time spent scrubbing counters and putting away dishes, and less time chatting with the neighbors or grabbing coffee with a friend.

Wouldn't it be wonderful to have a home you could clean in its entirety in just a few hours so that you could devote the rest of the weekend to enjoying time with your friends and family?

You might argue that your calendar *is* already filled. It's probably filled with scheduled appointments with other people—coffee dates, play dates, and violin practice all involve other people, so staying busy hasn't meant having no relationships. But what about your ability to emotionally *invest* in these people you love? Is your life slow enough to spend three hours over coffee, instead of one, because your friend pours out her heart to you about a struggle she's having? Is your calendar empty enough to accept a last-minute offer to have a cookout with your in-laws? When you're running errands, are you able to spend time chatting with your former professor you bumped into at the post office? By keeping our firm commitments to a minimum, we're saying "yes" to being available for people who enter our lives casually.

2. Improved Health

Our mental, emotional, and physical health is taking a serious toll because of our cluttered lives. We're stressed, we're easily overwhelmed, and we're not sleeping well because our homes are too crowded with stuff. We walk into our messy homes, and we're discouraged and defeated before we even start, not knowing where to begin.

As we strive to afford our hefty mortgages, it's nearly impossible to imagine life as a single-income family. How could you buy groceries?

More than 60 percent of American families are dual-income earning,[8] which means a lot of hours at the office and not many at home. And after a long day of work, it's rather disheartening to roll up your sleeves to straighten up the house or start dinner. But because we believe we need all these extracurricular commitments and gadgets to make our homes nicer, we must work long hours to afford and maintain it all. All of this work outside the home means stress inside the home, the one place that's meant to be your haven.

Hours and hours of housework usually result in an exhausted body. Who has the time to make a healthy meal from scratch, or to even enjoy those luxuries we're working so hard to have? It's not easy to manage a large floor plan with stuff on every available surface.

We're a rather sleep-deprived culture. Because of our long workdays, our evenings spent carting our kids to their activities, and the more than eight hours per day we spend as a family parked in front of the TV, we're going to bed late and then getting up early to start it all over again. Not enough sleep means an increased chance of depression, weight gain, high blood pressure, and perpetual grouchiness.

It truly is ironic that we don't have time to enjoy the gadgets and luxuries we can afford on a large income rewarded from long working hours. We spend much of our weekends catching up on laundry, running errands, and cleaning the neglected bathroom. It's a chain-link downward spiral: We want stuff, so we work hard; our hard work allows us to buy stuff, but our hard work takes all of our energy, so we can't enjoy our stuff as much as we would like.

A decluttered, simple home will remove much of your physical stress and exhaustion. You won't feel overwhelmed when you walk in the front door. Your relatively organized calendar will be easy to read and maintain. And you'll be able to guiltlessly kick up your feet and rest in your armchair, enjoying the few things you do have because you truly enjoy them all.

You will physically feel better when you get rid of those things you don't need.

3. Financial Well-Being

As a culture, we are spending *far* too much money—money that we often don't even have—on things we simply don't need. We never feel like we have enough money. Even when we budget every month and use a cash-envelope system, it seems like there's usually more month than money. But this shortfall usually occurs because we're spending and not saving.

If we free our homes of things we don't need, there's a good chance we'll earn at least a little cash if we choose to sell these things in a garage sale, on eBay, or on Craigslist. But we're also saving money down the road, because we don't need to maintain those things we never loved to begin with.

If we have less clutter, we can find the things we're looking for. A decluttered kitchen is a much saner place to prepare meals, which means less eating out and less money spent on bloated entrées at restaurants. When we toss the paperwork we don't need, we're able to find important papers, making it infinitely easier to pay bills on time, store useful coupons, and remember appointments without paying penalty fees.

And we shouldn't write off the emotional freedom that comes with decluttering our homes, which directly affects our financial wellbeing. It might be painful at first to sell the wedding gifts you never liked but felt guilty about tossing—but once you feel the weight lifted off your shoulders and see the glorious empty space in your closet, you might start snowballing this decluttering thing. You're more apt to remove the emotion from *things*, so it's easier to rid your home of all but what you love. Selling more things means earning and keeping more money, and keeps you from buying needless stuff in the future.

4. An Ecological Step in the Right Direction

Our landfills are overflowing. The vehicles we use to cart all of our stuff have created the worst air quality in history. It's not a scare tactic; it's the truth—if we want a decent life for ourselves, let alone our children's children, we must be *much* better stewards of our possessions. Our dependence on superfluous stuff has resulted in damage to our air, our local water, our soil, and our oceans, both for us and for our neighboring countries.

I'm not a hard-core, tree-hugging environmentalist. I'm just passionate about being good stewards of what God has given us. It's folly to balk at supporting ways to consume less fossil fuel—that's not being a green nut; that's caring about the impact oil production has on the Earth, lowering gas prices, and doing what we can to make life better for future generations.

When we get rid of the things we don't need and either donate them to charity or sell them secondhand, we're providing someone with a way to reuse something instead of buying it new. We're supporting the *reuse* part of the three-R mantra of environmentalism.

When our households have less stuff, we don't need as much space. Less space means lower utilities, which is both financially savvy and ecologically sound. You'll use less electricity, less gas, and less water to keep your place running.

You could even argue that decluttering your home means enjoying more of nature. Running a simpler home takes less time to clean, and you'll have more money freed up to use that time in your backyard or out and about.

Realistic simple living *is* for you and your family. It's the best way to live life. It means that all the parts of your life are pointed in the same direction, a direction that has purpose and vibrancy. So now that we've established that the *real* definition of simple living is *living holistically with your life's purpose*, let's explore the different ways you can find your direction and purpose.

3 | A Family Purpose Statement

Make Simple Living Personal

"First say to yourself what you
would be; and then do what
you have to do."

–EPICTETUS

I hate to break it to you, but you can't do it all. I can't either. We're all given a finite amount of time, resources, and talents, which makes it rather impossible to achieve that noble, yet impossible ambition of doing everything well that you want to do. It's simply not possible, and it's a poor use of energy and devotion. Seasons of life come and go, and with them ebb physical capabilities, levels of stamina, and free time. No one in the history of the world has been able to accomplish it all.

I'm a big believer in following the writer Elisabeth Elliot's advice, "When you don't know what to do next, just do the thing in front of you." But it certainly helps if you have more of an *idea* of what's the most important thing to do next.

In 1967, Charles E. Hummel wrote and published an essay entitled *Tyranny of the Urgent*, stating that the "greatest danger is letting the urgent things crowd out the important." We spend so much of our energy and time putting out fires, answering phone calls and e-mails, and in the meantime, we let the most important things in our life pass us by. In the twenty-first century, many of us respond to the tyranny of the urgent. We let the things we value most take a backseat to whatever is begging for attention in the moment.

One of the characteristics of a responsible adult is to recognize the difference between the important and the urgent, and then refuse to be tyrannized by the urgent—to shun management by crisis. Of course, this is easier said than done. Who hasn't tried to make dinner for the family (the important), but can't seem to find the time it takes because of an exploding diaper, spilled juice, or a ringing telephone (the urgent)?

In managing your home, you must know the difference. You cannot operate solely in response to the urgent for long—you'll go mad. And if your desire is to live simply, it's essential to know what's the most important stuff in life and what's, well, urgency disguised as importance.

So how do you decide *what* to do? Within a busy world and a fast-paced culture with an infinite list of demands, your soul needs some constant, a rock that helps you determine what you *can* do and what you just *can't*, or at least what can wait until later. This unshakable rock needs to be something that makes sense, that's clearly defined, and that is consistent with your priorities.

This is when a purpose statement proves invaluably handy. I'm not talking about a clichéd "mission statement," satirized in *Jerry Maguire* and in a stereotyped office atmosphere; I'm talking about a real, definitive, no-holds-barred statement that says what *you're* about. And if you're sharing a roof with other family members, I'm talking about a statement that says what *all* of you are about. The following advice is written for families of any size and shape, but it will work just as well for independent individuals. Apply the information to your current life stage.

What's a Purpose Statement?

There's no right or wrong way to word a purpose statement, but the statement should cover the overall picture of your life's purpose. Remember the definition of simple living?

Living holistically with your life's purpose.

In order to live simply, you need to *know* your purpose and write it in a statement. How do you discover your purpose? One way is to answer questions, discuss their answers, write down thoughts, and scratch out other ideas. This chapter will help you journey through a process of discovering more clearly what you—and your family—are all about. You'll identify your priorities, which will point you to your purpose. It won't be perfect because you're not perfect. No one is, so don't set unrealistic expectations.

In the end, the goal is to have a clear, concise, workable purpose statement that accurately reflects your priorities, your personality, and your vision for your family. You want it to be a timeless, easy-to-read, holistic statement that applies to everyone in the family. It will help you make decisions, feel confident about saying "no," and be a bit better at focusing on the important instead of the urgent.

And ultimately, this statement will clearly mark the road for your journey toward simple living. You will know what a simple life means to *you*, and it won't remain some vague, trendy buzzword that sounds lovely but means very little.

What Does a Purpose Statement Look Like?

As I mentioned, there's no right or wrong way to word a family purpose statement. It can be detailed, complete with bullet points, or it can be one word. Usually, something in the middle of those two extremes works best for most families. Here are the keys to crafting a statement that's useful enough to be put into practice.

1. It Should Be Simple

It's basic logic: A purpose statement with an end goal to simplify your life should be simple in itself. It shouldn't have five-dollar words, so many specifics that it's not pliable, or so many complexities that the children don't understand it. This is a tool for your family, not a doctoral thesis. Make it work for you and your family.

2. It Should Be Timeless

A family purpose statement is not the place to outline your goals for the year, nor to elaborate on the career hopes you have for your preschoolers. Ideally, your statement should be just as workable when your kids are five as when they're fifteen. You will have space elsewhere to elaborate on what your purpose statement looks like in your life right *now*, but those specifics don't belong in the statement itself. It doesn't need to be perfect, of course, and it's perfectly fine to tweak and remold the statement throughout the years as your family organically evolves. However, as you approach this project of crafting your statement, keep timelessness a priority.

3. It Should Be General, but Not Too General

Along the lines of timelessness, you also want to keep your statement rather general—but not so general that it doesn't accurately reflect who you are. For example, if you're passionate about environmentalism, you might be tempted to include, "Pioneer a movement of recycling in my neighborhood." This might be a bit too specific—that's more of a goal than a statement of purpose, anyway. But don't veer to the other spectrum and write only, "Love the earth." That doesn't really speak about your specific niche within the big vision of loving the earth, nor does it spark any creativity and inspiration for your future decision making. Find the balance between specific and general. In this case, something like, "Steward the earth locally while mobilizing environmental change globally" might better fill the bill. If it's too vague, it won't really help in your day-to-day decision making. If it's too specific, it may needlessly paint you into a corner you never intended.

Real-Life Examples From Real Families

For further inspiration, I've collected a few family purpose statements from actual families. I don't want these to define how your statement will ultimately look, but perhaps they'll spark an idea or a vision as you craft your own.

Here is my family's purpose statement:

As a family, we want to glorify God in all we say, do, and are. We will …

- Put each other first.
- Cultivate deep relationships with one another.
- Extend love to those around us.
- Live simply.
- Be true to who God made us.
- Take care of our health.
- Be good stewards of creation.
- Be lifelong learners.

MaryJo Wieland, writer at TurnItUpMom.com and wife and mom of one child in New Jersey, has defined her family's purpose statement as:

- Kindness: Generosity of Spirit. We show people that we care. We are sympathetic and understanding, and we act with a warm heart.

- Responsibility: We have a responsibility to ourselves, to our communities, and to the world.
- Faith: We believe in God and in each other. We are loyal to each other, trusting that each person has something special to offer the world.
- Fun: We remember to approach life with a light-hearted playfulness, to laugh a lot, and to make memories together.

Lisa Delzer, a wife and mom of two small children in Colorado, shared with me her family's purpose statement:

We believe that our purpose as a family is to love, celebrate, and nourish the creative spirit. We will accomplish this by:
- living simply, loving unconditionally, and exploring
- making our home a place of creativity, laughter, and love
- valuing the creative process above all else, and
- being in harmony with Spirit, each other, and Mother Nature.

Kara Fleck, editor of SimpleKids.net and wife and homeschooling mom of three living in Indianapolis, has a very simple but powerful purpose statement:

To be focused on *peace*.

Now It's Your Turn

Ready to get to work? Set aside time on your calendar with your spouse (or yourself if you are single)—a quiet evening where you'll have a couple of hours over cups of tea to talk and write together. It doesn't need to be long, but you might need to schedule a few sessions if each one is short on time. Take your time devising this purpose statement.

Pick the questions here that resonate most with you, and jot down some thoughts. If you are an individual, modify the questions so they apply to you. Don't worry about right or wrong answers. Write the first answer that comes into your mind, or simply write down some words that percolate as you mull over the topic.

1. What are a few strengths of each member of our family?
2. Collectively, we are at our best when we are …
3. Collectively, we are at our worst when we are …
4. If we had a completely free day together as a family, how would we spend it?
5. What are practical ways we can serve each other?
6. What are practical ways we can serve others outside our family?
7. Name three things we think we could do better as a family.
8. What would people say today about our family as a whole?
9. What would we like people to say about our family as a whole in thirty years?
10. If our home could be filled with one emotion, what would that emotion be?
11. Name three adjectives we would like people to use to describe our home environment.
12. If we could name one principle from which we want our family to operate, what would it be?
13. What are the top four priorities we want our family to value?
14. What is the main purpose of our home?
15. What is the secondary purpose of our home?

16. What is the individual purpose in life of each member of our family?
17. What is one way we are unique as a family?
18. Describe the status of our family in ten years …
    - financially:
    - intellectually:
    - emotionally:
    - relationally with each other:
    - communally in our environment:
    - physically:
    - spiritually:
19. Where are you as a family in ten years? What does your home look like?
20. What is the purpose of life?

What to Do With Your Answers

Look at your responses and see if there's a theme. If you repeatedly talk about making a difference in your community, perhaps you have that innate passion within you. Or if your priorities seem to point to being good stewards of the environment, maybe a priority for you is to leave the earth better than you found it. Notice trends in your answers.

Chat about your answers with your spouse. Do you differ on any of the answers? That could be a big deal, or it could be nothing. Either way, it should spark some discussion between the two of you.

Once you've settled on a few basic repeated themes, nail down a few descriptive words to encompass them. For example, if your answers repeatedly deal with being frugal, with not living among clutter, and having plenty of free time as a family, perhaps one of your descriptive words is *simplicity*.

Tweak some of your descriptors to be more timeless. For example, if your answer to question 12, about one principle from which your family operates, is "patience as we live through the baby and toddler years," you could discuss whether patience is a theme that's significant to both of you long-term. Perhaps one of your guiding principles is *forbearance*, which means patient endurance and self-control.

Create Your Statement

Start crafting a draft of your family purpose statement by way of your answers to the questions found earlier in this chapter. There's no right or wrong way to write this, but remember to keep it simple and timeless, and to create a fine balance between vague and specific. And keep it on the shorter side; if it's too long, it'll be difficult to remember.

If you're stuck on where to begin, you could try a skeleton like this:

We, the [family name], believe that our purpose as a family is to [general mission statement]. We will accomplish this by:

- valuing [principle] and [principle] as our main guiding principles
- making our home a place of [adjective], [adjective], and [adjective]
- prioritizing [value or action] above lesser values
- interacting with each other in a spirit of [adjective]

These questions, the outline, and everything in between are ideas to get you started. Be creative and original! Make this an adventure with your family, and see where it leads you. Let your statement reflect who you are as a family.

Most important, let your statement be one that will help guide you as you make future decisions—let it serve you as a family. It's a tool, not an altar where you worship. Keep the definition of simple living in mind—*living holistically with your life's purpose.* If this purpose statement can help you define your life's purpose, then you are a major step closer to realistic simple living.

Take It a Step Further

Once you've got a working purpose statement, feel free to use it to create goals that can be a bit more immediate. For example, if one of your main points is that you will "value simplicity as a family," you can jot down some ideas of what this looks like for you in the next year. For example, this could mean:

- We will operate from one income so that one spouse can stay home and have adequate time to manage our family effectively.
- We will only allow outside commitments three nights per week so that we have enough time at home as a family.
- We will eat out once every other week so that we have enough funds to take a small vacation each year.

The next two chapters discuss *how* your purpose statement can help you make wise daily financial choices and guard your precious time.

And as you begin to think about the implications of this purpose statement, you will be able to see how certain home management tasks will be a priority, while others won't be as important. It will wipe away some needless guilt about "doing it all," and it will further free you from a burden you were never meant to carry. Realistic simple living is about being true to yourself, knowing your limits, and embracing your gifts and passions.

Consider displaying your statement somewhere as an inspiration and encouragement when decision making is tough. It will send you out the door with a visible reminder of what you're about in your small corner of the big world. Jon and Cherie Werner in Austin, Texas, together with their three girls, wrote their statement with permanent marker on an inexpensive plate, which they display on a shelf in their living room.

Your family's purpose statement is a powerful tool. It is a major instrument in your quest to live against the grain of modern-day culture. When you second-guess your decisions or your priorities, you can read your purpose statement and be encouraged that simple living is worth it.

4 | Time Is a Tool

Use It Wisely; Enjoy It Thoroughly

"To choose time is to save time."

–FRANCIS BACON

Other than money, the biggest commodity that keeps you from living simply is time. You probably often wish you had more of both. Do you have plenty of overlapping activities, events, and circumstances competing for your attention? At the end of the day, you probably crash in bed exhausted at your life's obligations, even when you don't get everything on your to-do list completed. And then you wake up the next morning and start all over again.

So when I tell you now that you need *more* free time in your family's life, there's a good chance you're wondering *where* on earth you would even find some, let alone enjoy it. Who has any free time when you've got long work hours, an excess of afterschool activities for each child, extended-family expectations, and a home to maintain? And that's excluding essentials like eating, sleeping, exercising, and just moving from one event to another. If you even entertained such notions as homeschooling your kids, volunteering in the community, or starting a home-based business, you'd throw in the towel before you even started. Who has time for such pursuits?

Well, here's the thing—everyone has been allotted the same amount of time. We're all given twenty-four hours per day. The only difference in time between one person and another is how each person chooses to spend those same hours. Everybody is given the same chance, time-wise, to pursue different things. We each choose to spend those hours in a variety of different ways.

And because this means we've got finite time to do finite activities, it should be a given that we use that time wisely and intentionally. The wasting of time is a sad thing to witness. How much sadder would it be to waste it collectively as a family?

Finite time means you can't do everything, so a smart person would intentionally and selectively choose which things to spend time on and which ones to let pass. There should be some sort of criteria through which every potential event should pass, and it should only be added to the family calendar when it passes with flying colors. Doesn't sound too difficult. So why do most families feel absolutely overwhelmed at everything that's on their plate?

Why Families Are Too Busy to Simplify

There's never just one reason that a family is too busy; most excuses cross-pollinate and feed off each other. But if we were to list them, here are some of the main time eaters.

1. Too Much Screen Time

According to a recent survey done in the UK, more than a third of the one thousand families surveyed watch TV together for at least an hour every night, including weekends. Another 32 percent watch TV together two to three times a week. One in ten families feels that the pressures of work and home life means that time watching the TV is their only chance to bond. More than half of those surveyed find that parking in front of the tube together is the best way to catch up with each other, and 12 percent admitted that it's the only time the entire family is together in the same room.[9]

Does it strike you as a little odd that these families find that the best way to catch up with each other is to park in front of an appliance that shows images of other people living fictional lives? I do.

According to the Nielsen Company, the average American watches more than four hours of TV each day—that's twenty-eight hours per week, or two months of nonstop TV watching per year. In an eighty-year life, that person will have spent more than thirteen years glued to the tube. This same survey approximated that the average American youth spends nine hundred hours annually in school and 1,500 hours per year watching TV. Among parents surveyed, 73 percent admitted that they'd like their children to watch less television, but only 49 percent of American adults feel like they personally watch too much. Possibly most shocking, this same survey reported that parents admit to spending a total of three-and-a-half minutes per week in meaningful conversation with their child.[10]

Is there little wonder why most modern-day families feel too busy? They're apparently allowing television to take most free time they might have. Why on earth do we willingly hand over our physical health, our ability to self-entertain, and—most important in this chapter—our time to an electronic box, and then moan that we never have enough time?

The other screen that lures families into whittling away precious time is the computer. In this digital age, the computer serves as our main form of communication, our useful work tool, an educational service, and oftentimes our telephone and—yes—our television. A little more than 80 percent of all American homes have a computer, and more than 90 percent of these households have an Internet connection.[11]

As a blogger, I obviously don't mind the computer at all—until it dries up precious time for doing things like talking with my family, exercising, reading a book, and managing my home. I can easily fall prey to the computer's seductive lure, as many others do who work from home, thanks to the Internet. A study done by the Nielsen-funded Council for Research Excellence reported that the average American spends 143 minutes per day staring at their computer screen—that's about two-and-a-half hours. That may not seem like too much, until you consider that after combining it with vegging in front of the TV or dinking with some other gadget, we spend eight-and-a-half hours per *day* staring into a screen of some kind.

Any way you slice it, people in the modern era devote an exorbitant amount of time to their electronic screens.

Too Much Structured Time for Kids

I'm not bemoaning the idea of a family routine; I think it's critically important, and we'll get to that in a moment. Here, I'm referring to the classic trend we see in many middle-class families today: Mom serving as the taxi, and the kids being carted around from every official activity the family can afford, be it Boy Scouts, violin practice, Little League, or even a simple playdate. Kids in today's generation have nowhere *near* the amount of free time their parents and grandparents enjoyed in their childhood. Climbing trees, building forts, and lazy days reading a book have been replaced with improving talents for that lofty college application. I wonder what our children's memories will be when they reflect on their upbringing—an innocent time full of play and exploration, or the booster seat on the way to ballet practice?

I'm not denouncing these activities—truly. I'm referring to the *amount* of time spent on these extracurriculars compared to the time devoted to just being a kid. In *Last Child in the Woods*, Richard Louv says, "It takes time—loose, unstructured dreamtime—to experience nature in a meaningful way. Unless parents are vigilant, such time becomes a scarce resource, because time is consumed by multiple invisible forces; because our culture currently places so little value on natural play."[12] Louv reports statistics that reveal that between 1981 and 2003, children have lost nine hours of discretionary time per week.

This means that between school, sleep, and homework, kids now have about twelve hours per week to enjoy a simple childhood. Once you add extracurricular activities to the mix, you can easily subtract four from that twelve. Eight hours a week—including weekends— doesn't devote much time to being a kid.

This, naturally, affects the entire family. Together, a family works to transport each other to their destinations, and schedules are arranged so that members can devote the needed time to each task while still managing to make it under the same roof each night. Even just one child's hyperstructured schedule can affect the whole family—and ultimately, a family's quest for a simpler life.

Work

And finally, a job is one of the major time eaters for an average adult. Work is good, and almost everyone must work in order to receive an income. But how many hours spent on the job, commuting to the job, or doing some form of preparation for that job (continuing education at a conference, buying the right clothes for the workplace, and driving to childcare so that the children are taken care of) are necessary? Where's the line dividing reasonable and overkill?

There's not a clear-cut answer, obviously, and different occupations demand different devotions of time. But it is clear from studies that Americans spend more hours working than just about any other nationality. According to the Center for Economic and Policy Research, the United States is one of the only industrialized countries that has no minimum paid-leave law. Most European countries have mandatory four- to five-week vacation standards. Australia has four, and the Japanese receive two. Americans have none—in fact, only 14 percent take a vacation in any given year.[4] We put more hours into our jobs than we did in 1950, and on average, we annually work 350 hours more than Europeans. That totals nine extra weeks on the job.[13]

Working hard is good, but so is working *smart*. There's a difference between logging a plethora of hours at work and working well. And when we give too many hours to our employer, our families suffer most. According to the National Institute of Child Health and Human Development, more and more children are cared for by people other than their parents, and older children are more likely today to come home to an empty house and spend time with their screens, with less guidance to offset or control the messages coming from these sources.[14] And because more than 60 percent of American households with children under age eighteen have both parents employed outside the home,[8] it's no wonder we're so busy spinning our wheels trying to maintain our home life.

What All of This Means

Putting it bluntly, most people are too busy to live simply. They are overcommitted, overworked, and overentertained by passive activities.

Living simply requires devotion to the task, and if you don't put in the hours to transform your life into something more meaningful and holistic with your life's purpose, it will never happen. Simple living doesn't happen automatically.

It's probably a common misconception that once you choose to live more simply, it will be easy to do so because it involves a lot of *not* doing something. How hard is it to simply not watch too much television? To not log too many working hours? It's pretty difficult, actually. Once you believe the commonplace notion that the definition of success is more stuff, it's hard to deliberately choose to jump off the hamster wheel and move at a slower pace. It feels strange to not be busy—most of us buy into the idea that to be busy is a barometer for productivity and that something's wrong if we're not.

Because the definition of simple living is *living holistically with your life's purpose*, simple living requires a change in definition of your life's purpose. The only way you'll have enough time to live mindfully and deliberately, congruent with what you want most in life (as described in your family purpose statement), is if you say "no" to those things that are incongruent.

But how? How do you know what things require a "no," while others are permitted through the gate? It can be tricky, but it's not impossible.

Making Priorities in Your Everyday Life

Take a moment to list everything you'd *like* to enjoy each month, but currently aren't doing. Your list can be a bit idealistic, but don't live in la-la land. No lounging at the pool eight hours a day, flying to a different country each week, or getting a daily massage at the nearby spa. Think of things that might *actually* be possible in your current life but aren't on the calendar for whatever reason.

Some of these might include:

- exercise
- get a full night's sleep
- read more books
- enjoy a particular hobby
- garden
- have a friend over for an afternoon coffee break
- join a book club, a Bible study, or some other community group
- volunteer at your favorite charity
- host a playgroup at home for your kids
- leisurely explore a specific part of your city
- regularly watch a particular TV show
- start a blog
- start a home-based business
- go on a regular date with your spouse

Now make another list. Catalog all the basic tasks you think you *need* to do to live. We're talking absolute basics. Some examples are:

- sleep
- eat three meals daily
- bathe
- work
- drive to certain places
- send kids to school or homeschool the kids
- cook

- clean the house
- do laundry
- pay bills

Now make a third list, this time noting all the things you do in an average month. Include everything—from sleeping to paying bills to watching TV and everything in between. List the fun stuff and the not-so-fun stuff. Some examples are:

- sleep
- eat three meals a day
- snack about twice a day
- watch TV
- check e-mail
- drive to work
- pick up kids from school
- take kids to afterschool activities
- surf the Internet
- window-shop at the mall
- balance the checkbook
- look for keys

You get the idea. You don't need to be fanatical, but be as thorough as possible. Stop when your head starts spinning.

Now lay all three lists side by side. Circle the items on your third list that aren't present on the other two. Those are the potential time-eating culprits. Can you assign a general time allotment per week to these tasks? For instance, would you guess you watch about two hours of TV each night? If so, put fourteen total hours per week next to "watch TV." How long is your work commute? If it takes you thirty minutes to get there and one hour in traffic to get home, then put 7.5 hours by "drive to work." How much sleep are you getting each night?

If you're like most people, you'll probably be stingy with your time allocations. You're probably honestly not aware of how much time you *do* spend watching TV—what feels like a few minutes could very well be hours. If you guesstimate watching two hour-long shows, the news, and a thirty-minute rerun before heading to bed with a late night talk show on in the background, you've logged almost four hours in just one evening. That's about twenty-eight hours a week on average.

Changing Your Habits

Change has got to start somewhere. You could divide poor time stewardship into roughly two categories: bad habits and too many events. Tackling habits is a challenge because it takes real work to make lasting change. Simple living is an active process, not a passive lifestyle goal— it's worth transforming bad habits into good ones, with the reward being more free hours for you to spend wisely.

Free Time

Imagine with me, for a moment, that you decided that there are three TV shows per week that you truly enjoy. These are shows that you're bummed to miss, that you want to catch before someone spills the ending to you. Hopefully you and your spouse agree on these, but that's not always the case. Between the two of you, maybe you could aim for no more than five unmissable shows. If you were to watch only these five shows, you'd watch approximately three to five hours of television per week, with a total of twenty hours logged at most in an average month. That's twenty hours in one month, instead of the typical 112 hours most Americans spend watching TV per month. Do you think the ninety-two hours earned per month would allow you to slow down, to pursue some hobbies, to exercise, or to get some much-needed sleep?

There's the added bonus that your television watching will become more of an event, and therefore more enjoyable. You could pop popcorn, dim the lights, settle in on the couch with a comfy blanket, and sit together as a couple or a family—instead of having the boob tube mindlessly blaring in the background as you rush around doing other activities or, even worse, spacing out.

It's worth your health and your time to cut back on TV watching. Don't sacrifice precious hours to watching what happens with other people's lives, either real or fictitious, when you've got your own life to live. Your family's well-being is too valuable.

You could also add loafing around as a popular habit. Along with watching TV, many of us spend time browsing the Internet, putzing around the house, window-shopping, flipping through magazines and catalogs, and let's not forget one of America's favorite pastimes, mall crawling. None of these things are terribly awful; it's just that many of these things are performed lackadaisically, without much thought for the how, the why, and the when. There's a big difference between intentional downtime and spacing out, and in a contest, intentional downtime wins hands down. We should recharge our batteries, relax, and get refreshed doing those things we love best.

We'll get to the nitty-gritty of scheduling in a moment, and it's here that you'll schedule in some quality, intentional downtime. You can't *not* have downtime in life because you'll run on fumes and putter out with no energy or motivation. But think of those things you listed earlier in your list of things you'd like to do each month. Instead of checking out the mall scene as a way to distract from life's busyness, how about grabbing coffee with a friend? Perhaps you could curl up with a book on your reading list instead of flipping through magazines you don't really care about anyway. Or maybe even stroll through the mall, but with your spouse on the way to a restaurant on a date. It's important to write in downtime on the family calendar. But it's also important to use that time to really recharge and not just kill time.

Work

I hesitate to mention working as a habit because most of us need to work, both for financial obligations and for satisfaction. But I could argue that having *both* spouses begrudgingly employed outside the home even though it's not needed, or working a dead-end job that leaves you unfulfilled, is a bad habit. We've seen the charts that show how little a dual-income family truly earns once you subtract the necessary expenses required for maintaining both jobs. There is a simple chart in appendix C to help you crunch some numbers. Fill it in with data from your life, and consider whether you truly need both parents to work. Working outside the home might be a necessary evil for some of us, but I'd argue that's the case for fewer of us than we assume. We will discuss money matters in much more detail in chapter 5.

Consider your options. Can you work from home? Could you start a home-based business? How about even cutting back your hours? It might take sacrifice, but think of what you're sacrificing in order to have a dual income—time. If you didn't work, what could you get done around the house, with your children, and with your personal interests?

And finally, you might still need to work, but where you're currently employed might be a drain in some form. Are you (or your spouse) having to work long hours with little pay to show for it? Is your job on the other side of town, which means a long commute in standstill traffic? Are your hours spent working on things that drain you and squelch your fire? Maybe this job is just a habit. You've been doing it so long that you can't imagine doing anything else or you really don't like it, but it takes too much work to find something else.

Be a responsible adult, but do what you can to make your employment work for you. Look over your family purpose statement. What speaks to your heart?

Making the Family Calendar Work

Okay, let's say that you've cut back your television time considerably, you've nixed a couple of extracurriculars from your kids' busy schedules, you enjoy downtime doing things you truly love and that energize you, and your work is meaningful and income generating. (Even if you're at home, working primarily as a home manager, your job can be seen as income generating if it allows your spouse to work outside the home freely and if it saves your family money.) Then what? There's still the question of how to schedule your life and how to know what stays and what goes.

There must be some form of criteria. We've already established that simple living is an active pursuit, and this is evident in the family calendar as well. You can't let all others dictate what event *has* to be attended because you'll never have a moment to yourself as a family. Here are a few guidelines for deciding whether an event or a routine is worth your precious time.

Does It Line Up With Your Family Purpose Statement?

First and foremost, it has to be congruent with your family's desires; otherwise you're not living simply. Remember the definition of simple living—*living holistically with your life's purpose.* If you're spending valuable time on an activity that doesn't really fulfill your family's purpose, then you're taking away time from events that *would* fulfill your purpose and, therefore, add more meaning to your life.

Let's say that one of the items in your family's purpose statement is to show kindness to others. One week you're faced with a schedule conflict—do you attend that in-home product demonstration party your friend is hosting, or do you finally have your neighbors over for dinner, the new family you've been meaning to get to know for months? You could argue that either event could be showing kindness. But which event would you guess would have more meaning to the recipient: your attendance at the party or preparing and hosting a meal for your new neighbors? It may depend on the friend, but I'd guess having your neighbors over for dinner would hold more meaning, both for your family and for your guests. You'd be extending love to people who are possibly aching for some new friends, and you'd be fulfilling one of your family's chief purposes. That's meaningful for both sides.

Your party-hosting friend might be offended, but that leads us right to the next criterion.

Are You Doing It to Make Others Happy?

How often do you begrudgingly attend an event or participate in an activity just so someone else would be pleased? How much energy and precious time is spent making others happy, all the while you're left busy, exhausted, and bitter? There's one *you* (or four or five, depending on the size of your family) and about six billion *others*—you'll be busy for a long while if you value pleasing people.

Let's use the example of your friend's party. If she were truly a friend, most often a phone call and an explanation would satisfy a responsible, mature decline to attend. If she were to take offense at your well-justified reason, then perhaps your mother's sage proverb still holds true—maybe she wasn't a real friend after all. If you attend the party even though you don't want to, you're making someone else happy at the expense of your own peace.

Now, I'm not talking about getting your way in life in all circumstances, no matter what. There are times when the mature thing to do would be to attend that party, even if it's not your first choice on how to spend the evening. But if going to functions out of obligation becomes a habit, you and your family won't be too happy long-term.

What about extended family? Now there's a category of people that's far too easy to feel guilty over. How do you decide where you'll spend the holidays? Perhaps you alternate family sides, with each side getting either Thanksgiving or Christmas each year, and then next year it's reversed. If that satisfies your extended family *and* you, then all's well. But if you're employing this system because that's the way it's always been done and because your mother's feelings would really be hurt if you didn't show, then you're asking for frustration and bitterness.

As a single-family unit, you might need to construct some intentional boundaries to your valuable space and time. You're an adult. If it's financially and emotionally best for your immediate family to stay in town for Christmas this year, then a wise, empathetic grandparent should understand that. It doesn't happen often, I know. But if you've approached this tactic maturely with other people's feelings considered, then the bitterness should fall on their shoulders, not yours. Don't risk your immediate family's peace so that your parents or in-laws can be momentarily happy.

Is It Really Necessary?

Some events aren't fun, and on the surface they don't appear to really line up with your overall purpose in life, but they've just got to happen, and they benefit you long term. Your son's parent–teacher conference. Your annual checkup at the doctor. The weekend work conference.

But there are some events that we've treated as *musts*, but really, they're optional. You don't really need to join the PTA—no one's holding a gun to your head (though it might feel that way when the PTA president calls!). If your child is sick, then the Sunday school picnic might just need to be skipped this time. Do you have to go shopping for a wedding shower present, or can you order something online through the couple's registry?

Don't give an activity a higher priority than it deserves.

Is It Simply Part of Your Current Season of Life?

Sometimes we just have to roll with life's punches and spend more time on something we don't love while spending less time on something we do. It's not ideal, but it's just the way things are for a short, concentrated season of life. Perhaps you have a newborn, so getting eight hours of uninterrupted sleep per night is impossible. Or maybe your son's stellar baseball skills ushered him into a summer on the all-star baseball team, meaning several nights per week cheering him on in the stands.

So long as it's a season, be at peace with the fact that it will pass. You can soon rearrange your time allocations so that they better reflect your values. This means saying no to something even though you would like to say yes. It's necessary because your current season simply does not allow it.

Don't let your current season-of-life activities morph into long-term habits, or you will be guilty of letting the urgent things replace the important. But flexibility is the key here, which means ebbing and flowing with life's changes.

As Jamie Martin, editor of SimpleHomeschool.net and mom of three, says in her book *Steady Days*:

"I often remind myself that flexibility is the key to enjoying the early years of life with young children. … Life with little ones is always evolving. Just when you think you have something figured out, the entire game plan changes, the phase passes, and there's something new to tackle."

Seasons of life pass, which means our daily routines will need to continually evolve.

Do You Have the Time?

Finally, when push comes to shove, you have to decide if you can allot the required time for an event. Is it worth the points on college applications to have your child enrolled in baseball, football, tennis, and piano lessons if he doesn't get enough sleep? Are you able to join the neighborhood book club if it's held on the same night that your husband works late? Remember, we're all given twenty-four hours in a day. There is not enough time for all the things you want to do, especially if you want to do them well.

The Nitty-Gritty

What does using time intentionally look like in a family setting? Here are a few tips for making the most of your time together.

- Jot down events on the calendar as soon as you receive the invitation. Don't let them linger in your head.
- Once a week, have an appointment with your spouse, and go over the upcoming week's calendar of events. Talk through items of importance, organize pick-ups and attendance, and find out how you can serve one another this week.
- Create a rough weekly routine. Write it in pencil because it will change, but create one nonetheless, so you have a framework upon which you can hang appointments. You can copy the basic weekly schedule in appendix C.
- Turn what is usually just downtime into events. As mentioned earlier, downtime must be essential. If you really want some relaxing time this week, write it down. "Reading time" or "sewing" is just as vital as "dentist appointment." If you don't have specific plans yet, still block out that chunk of time as filled so that you don't needlessly fill the calendar to the brim.

- Decide on an event quota. Between you and your spouse, one of you is bound to have a more sensitive threshold of sanity when it comes to events. My husband really doesn't like to have events planned more than three nights a week, so I try to honor that and not insist on more than is necessary for him. Find what works for both of you. If one of you wants more people time than the other, perhaps the introvert can stay home and soak up some precious alone time, while the extrovert can enjoy coffee with friends.

Time is a tool. You've got a limited amount, and it doesn't stop for you to catch your breath. Align your habits and your lifestyle with your purpose in life so that you're running at a comfortable pace and gliding along with time, rather than wishing it would slow down. A simple life values time and uses it well.

5 | Money Is a Tool

Steward It Well

"There is no dignity quite so impressive, and no independence so important, as living within your means."

–CALVIN COOLIDGE

As you begin the journey to a more simplified life, you might be wondering how much it's going to cost. It's rather ironic, isn't it? Sometimes it seems like simplifying and decluttering costs *more* than living in a more shortcut route. That's only true *if* you believe the marketing schemes.

Organizing is a billion-dollar industry. There are stores dedicated to selling things to hold your things, and you could buy a truckload of organizing supplies that do little more than add to the clutter—they just help you organize the clutter you still have. The Container Store alone averages a revenue of 650 million dollars a year. I like the store, in theory, but the fact that this chain can grow 20 percent per year[15] and sell thousands of products dedicated to—well, containing things—is telling. It says that people are drawn to things that make their lives simpler, more streamlined, and more organized, and that they are willing to pay big money on the bet that these items will do the trick.

Simple living is a state of mind. It's a choice to not let the consumer-driven culture dictate how you live, what you invest in, and how you spend your valuable resources. And this choice of worldview should emanate in every facet of your life, including your wallet. The way you handle your finances and the transactions in your bank account should reflect your convictions about life. Do they?

Before you toss me aside with stomach-churning guilt, or before you assume I'm suggesting selling it all and living in the woods as a hermit, hear me out. It's okay to invest in things that really matter. It's fine to buy a four-dollar coffee every now and then. It's okay to occasionally dine in a restaurant. My family does all of those things.

The key difference is to *plan* to do those things, to deliberately set aside some funds that you can afford for the purpose of enjoyment. A family that embraces simple living controls their money, and they don't let whims or moods dictate how they spend it. This philosophy lets them truly enjoy those little pleasures that cost them hard-earned cash.

I'm not a financial guru, so I'm not qualified to give you specific advice on saving, investing, and reducing debt. But I *am* a home manager, and I'm fairly competent at handling our family's finances. My husband and I make thorough choices about where our money goes, which lets us drastically simplify our lifestyle without sacrificing its quality.

But I'm Not a Math Person

Neither am I. Ask my parents, and they'll tell you that I was so right-brained as a child it was almost disarming. Math has always been my least-favorite subject, and to this day, it's rather ridiculous how much I rely on a calculator for fairly simple equations. I'm telling you this to encourage you that you *can* handle your family's finances. You can keep track of where your money goes. You may even grow to enjoy it, as I now do. You don't need to have a degree in accounting or business, and you don't need to fully understand stock market reports.

Do you have a brain? A calculator? A bank account? Then you can manage your money. Congratulations on your qualification for living a simplified life that lets your bank account reflect your values.

How Does Money Stuff Relate to Simple Living?

It is infinitely easier to practice simple living when you don't have any debt. Debt means enslavement to the past, no matter how much you want to plan well for the future and live according to your own standards today. Unless you're free from the bondage of paying for your past, you can't responsibly live in the present and plan for the future. Living simply means choosing to invest in what's most important to you, shunning the rest, and making your home and life work to those ends. You can't do that well if you have debt.

It doesn't really matter what financial plan you use to get out of debt, so long as you can make it *your* family's plan, and so long as you understand that no debt is "good" debt. Getting out of debt is a primary step toward simple living. The sooner you are debt free, the sooner you can truly savor a simple life.

How to Pay Off Debt

We used a simple method of paying off our debts one at a time by putting a large amount of cash toward one debtor while paying only the minimums on the rest. We listed our debts in order from smallest to largest, and in our monthly budget, we allocated every last available cent toward paying the debt at the top of the list. After we blasted that small debt out of the water, we moved on to the next debt, which continued to get its minimum payment, *plus* all the money we allocated for the debt we just paid. And because there was more money headed to that debt, it was eliminated even more quickly, rolling on and on until we were at our last debt, throwing every bit of money to that one final bill. This method is often called "snowballing." We reached our goal of becoming debt-free much faster than we anticipated, and now we don't owe a dime to anyone.

In the back of this book, I've listed resources that provide more information and specific guidance on using this method to get out of debt.

Budgeting: It's All About Choices

Even when you're debt-free, you'll still have a finite amount of money in your bank account. Not many of us can boast an endless supply of cash, so unless your last name is Gates or Trump, assume you'll need to allocate your money so that the well doesn't run dry.

What's simple living to one family might look like something entirely different to another. You might care a great deal more about traveling than another family, who has a higher priority of going to local concerts and museums. Both are fine, but the trademark quality in both of these families' decisions is *contemplation*. A lot of thought went into each spending decision, and the families' finances reflect this thought. This is budgeting.

Don't assume your money will automatically be spent where it should because it doesn't have a mind of its own. Cash is a tool, and it needs to be treated as such. Use it wisely to build, to repair, and to create the things that matter most to you.

The simplest definition of a budget is "telling your money where to go." I like that. It quells the fear behind this oft-feared word, and it relieves the reluctant free spirit who's afraid that living by a budget means boredom and bondage.

When you live by a budget, you're free to allocate the money where you have a need. After first budgeting the essentials, budget the extras you crave—such as a weekly latte. If something is a priority for you, then by all means, budget it in. Don't buy in to the rumored notion that a budget is about stripping away all pleasures.

I prefer using a zero-based budget, which simply means the income minus the expenses equals zero. There's no "leftover" money, because the money is allocated to a specific line item, even if that line item is as vague as "free-spending" money. A zero-based budget doesn't mean you have to spend all of your money each month. You can easily build savings into this model by counting your planned savings amount as an expense.

I also recommend using "sinking funds" for payments that do not occur monthly. For example, if you pay your auto insurance quarterly, simply set aside funds each month for the total annual amount of your insurance premium, divided by twelve. Many online banks allow you to have limitless savings accounts, so you can label each account with its corresponding sinking fund and have the money automatically transferred to this account each pay period. This makes the sinking fund process streamlined and simple.

Page 74 shows an extremely simplified example of a family working the "debt snowball" to pay off their debt, using a zero-based budget and sinking funds for irregular expenses.

You'll notice I subtract charitable giving right way. In my opinion, charitable giving should be deducted from your pay before you budget. So if you like to give 10 percent to your local church, I recommend having that amount automatically transferred to a sinking fund labeled "giving" within twenty-four hours of your employer's direct deposit. Then proceed with budgeting, using 90 percent of your salary as your income.

Head to appendix C to find a basic zero-based budgeting worksheet you can enlarge and copy.

SOURCE	AMOUNT
Monthly Income	
Paycheck (minus giving)	$3500.00
Work reimbursement	$59.50
Birthday gift	$75.00
Total income	$3634.50
Regular Monthly Expenses	
Mortgage	$1,000.00
Utilities	$100.00
Home insurance	$83.00
Groceries	$300.00
Health insurance	$200.00
Debt snowball	$1000.00
Gasoline	$200.00
Cell phone	$80.00
Internet	$50.00
Spending money	$60.00
Irregular Monthly Expenses	
School supplies/ books	$12.50
Christmas	$42.00
Clothing	$42.00
Gifts	$25.00
Haircut	$20.00
Household supplies	$20.00
Health insurance deductible	$167.00
Auto insurance premium	$150.00
Auto insurance deductible	$83.00
Total expenses	$3634.50
Minus income	-$3634.50
Equals	$0

Saving to Stay Debt-Free

Retirement doesn't pay for itself, nor does higher education, nor a vacation. If you truly want to live simply, enjoying the ability to live in the moment while still preparing for life down the road, you'll need to save money. Make saving money a nonnegotiable necessity in your budget. You'll have the freedom to take a family vacation, pay for a car in cash, or even build a modest dream home without being enslaved to the bank.

It takes sacrifice, for sure. It won't work well unless you save deliberately for specific goals and have particular numbers in mind. It'll require you to say no to many things that don't matter but sure do look good. But if you're committed to living simply, you should already have the conviction that part of a quality life is saying no to the things that don't matter so that you can say yes to the things that do. Living holistically with your life's purpose applies to your finances, too.

Being debt-free means you are free to save money. And saving money is a crucial part of simple living, because it allows you to live life on your terms, making choices that make sense to *you*. When debt dictates where your money goes, it's pretty hard to live holistically.

Just as becoming debt-free requires a plan, effectively saving money requires a plan as well. Think thoroughly about the things for which you need to save, and take the steps necessary to make that money grow for you.

Saving for Emergencies

In today's economy, no one can float through life without a financial safety net. If you've sworn off credit cards and become debt-free, you need accessible cash for emergencies because emergencies *will* happen.

It's commonplace to rely on credit cards when the transmission blows, but that's not an option when you don't allow credit cards into your life. It's so much simpler, so much more reliable, and so much freer to pay cash.

After you've become debt-free, continue making the same payment, only pay it to your own savings account. Instead of paying for the past, you'll be saving for the future, for when those storm clouds approach your life. You'll be surprised at how quickly your account will fill, especially if you don't raise your standard of living from when you were paying off debt.

It's wise to save at least three to six months of living expenses, veering closer to the six months side. You don't need to save six months' worth of *income*, only expenses. In a true emergency, you need funds for things like car repairs, mortgage payments, and groceries, not for dining out and vacations.

Saving for the Future

Along with emergencies, you need to save long term for the future. Saving for retirement is the most important investment you can make because no one else can do it for you. If you'd like to live out your golden years with dignity, then you shouldn't rely on your adult children and certainly not on the government. Make it an absolute priority to put aside funds each month into a pretax savings plan, such as a 401(k), or into a tax-free savings plan such as an Individual Retirement Account (IRA).

It's also a good idea to save for your children's future. Doing so would be a blessing for them, but keep in mind that a fully funded higher education is not their entitlement. Do not sacrifice your retirement for your child's university goals, because again, no one but *you* can save for your retirement. But if you are financially able, accessible money for tuition and books is a great reward for a responsible student who has earned your trust over the years.

If you're American, the best ways to save for education are through a Coverdell Education Savings Account or through your state's 529 plan. To learn more about saving for retirement and higher education, head to the resources section in the back of this book.

Saving for Wants

Lastly, being debt-free means you can save for some pleasures as well. Money is always a limited resource, and you'll never be able to have it all. But with some foresight and planning, you can enjoy some things that you'd truly appreciate.

Take a moment to jot down a few of your bigger dreams. Would you like to buy a house? A car? Would you love to take your family on a European vacation? How about some of those smaller pleasures, such as a great pair of jeans or a weekend away with your spouse? All of these things are good—but they're only good when you have the means to pay for them. Vacations are so much more enjoyable when you go on the trip knowing it's already paid for in full. Don't let your most memorable souvenir be a huge debt to repay. So after you've saved up a solid, six-month cushion for emergencies, specifically set aside funds for a few things on your want list.

Determine the total amount you'd like to save, divide it by the number of months between now and when you'd like to see this goal happen, and deposit this monthly payment into a savings account. Many banks (especially online banks) now allow unlimited savings accounts, so you can create different accounts for each savings goal. Separating your sinking funds like this keeps you from accidentally spending money, and you can much more easily track your financial progress.

You don't need a Spartan lifestyle, but you can't save well if you fritter away hard-earned cash on daily lattes, sales at big discount stores, or yard sale tchotchkes you never liked to begin with. One of the best side effects to financial progress is increased inner maturity, and part of this inner maturity is learning the value of saying "no." When you see how much those little things here and there add up, it's much easier to pass on the momentary satisfaction the purchase would bring. Such is the simple life. It all depends on your family's priorities and choices.

My Financial Story

As I said, you don't have to be an economics genius to make your money work for you. And you don't have to have a perfect, debt-free record to get your finances on track. You can start anywhere with any skill level. My parents taught me how to balance my checkbook when I opened my first checking account at age sixteen, but I learned little else about money management. I worked my way through college (in a local twenty-four-hour restaurant, often on the morning shift), eking by on the bare minimum. Saving was the last thing on my mind; I figured that was something people do when they graduate or when they have kids. I was a good student and mostly responsible, but I lived in the moment. I didn't blow my money on beer, but I wasn't exactly frugal, either.

I never really took the time to manage the money I *did* earn, so I graduated with a pretty strong work ethic, a pretty lousy grasp of money management, and a chain of school loans. I started working full time, but I still saved zero. It was never a priority. What was there to save for? I had never done it before, so why start now? I had enough for a decent apartment, I gave some to my church, and I could hit up the grocery store weekly. Because I wanted to work in the nonprofit industry, serving the underprivileged and making a difference worldwide, I even bought into the notion that saving money was something you did only if you loved money. I never had dreams of luxury living, so I wrote off saving money as though I just wasn't cut out for it. I continued to live in the moment.

Yes, it's ridiculous to assume that, in some magical way, those school loans would pay for themselves, even while working in full-time ministry and living below the American poverty line—but I did, and it was irresponsible. I also believed the popular lie that school loans are just something you always have, and because the interest rate is so low, it's not a big deal to have them.

Fast-forward a few years. My husband and I were newlyweds, basking in that early marriage glow in a tiny apartment with hand-me-down furniture. Life was good, and we were in love. But we were poor. We had zero money-management skills, and it felt like we had holes in our wallets—we had no idea where our money went. We didn't understand how our friends were able to save money while we couldn't, and we often prayed our way to the end of the month, hoping we'd have enough food to last until the next payday.

But I never looked myself square in the eye and took responsibility for my lack of money management. I always blamed it on the income side of the equation, reasoning that if we could just earn more, we'd be okay. I assumed everyone made way more than we did (which was mostly true), and that because we *meant* well with our money and didn't throw it away, we had just run into professional bad luck.

As I mentioned in chapter 1, my husband and I knew we wanted to live overseas from the beginning of our marriage. But we also knew we wanted to be debt-free before we made that journey, and at that point, debt was the main thing keeping us stateside. We couldn't live our life on *our* terms, because any extra money we had went to our debt. Lack of financial planning meant we were unable to live simply, on our terms.

I'll spare you the details, but with long hours and hard work, we paid off all but a few thousand dollars on our school loans. We finally moved overseas, four-and-a-half years into our marriage, with most of our debt gone. We weren't sure *how* we would pay the rest off, but we figured it would eventually happen.

One morning soon after our move, I was reading a blog post by my friend Crystal Paine, who writes at MoneySavingMom.com. She was sharing her family's progress in saving money for a 50 percent down payment on a home (they have since saved up to put 100 percent down—a house paid for in cash, essentially). I was blown away that anyone could do that, let alone Crystal and her young family—I knew she and her husband were in their mid-twenties (which was younger than us), and they had small children, too. What was her secret? She linked to the Web site of her favorite financial planning expert, Dave Ramsey, so I followed the link and devoured his site. And then I understood. I introduced my husband to this plan, and together we jumped on the debt-free wagon. For more information about Ramsey's plan, head to the resources section in the back of this book.

I'm elated to say that today we are not only debt-free, we also have a fully funded emergency fund, we have plans for retirement and savings for our kids' futures, and we are on a solid, workable blueprint that holistically combines our passion for living simply with our wallets. We have the means to live in a manner that we want right now, and we are on track with saving for the lifestyle we want in the future. And we're doing this on a very small income.

Living simply isn't always about going the cheapest route—it's about making choices. But it's hard to make these freeing choices that align with your family's heart when you're in bondage to debt. Choose to become a responsible adult in your household, and reclaim your right as a money manager. Make your money work for *you*, not you for it. Take the slower, temporarily more painful route of paying off your debt, and at the end of the journey, you'll find a light-ensconced field of freedom awaiting you. It's worth it.

6 | A Gathering Place

Create a Home Management Notebook

"Our life is frittered away by
detail ... Simplify, simplify."

−HENRY DAVID THOREAU

I'm sort of a minimalist by default, but it's still not easy to keep a well-organized, efficient, peaceful home when you've got three-foot mess makers running around. Or six-foot mess makers, for that matter. Sometimes, oftentimes, it can just get overwhelming.

This is when grace comes into play—giving heaps of it to yourself and your family members, remembering that the life stage of having children at home is so short. If you believe relationships are more important than a perfect house, you really can cut yourself some slack.

But you still need to keep up the house. Your current life stage—whatever it is—doesn't give you a "get-out-of-jail-free" card when it comes to home management. In fact, I find that the stage of raising a family makes it all the more important to find a management system that works well. Kids are happier in a home in which things have their place. Parents can hold onto a string of sanity when there's a tangible goal toward house cleaning, and at the end of the day, the family can relax in an actual haven, not a chaotic zoo.

My personal home management notebook is my lifeblood for giving me some direction, goals, and checklists for my job at home, and it's a great place to dump all the paperwork that you believe you need to keep but aren't quite sure where to put.

What's a Home Management Notebook?

It's easy to get overwhelmed by all the tasks necessary for running a household. There's laundry, bills, errands, cooking, parenting, even homeschooling for some. Add in making quality, laid-back family time a priority, and it's a full plate for any well-intentioned home manager.

A home management notebook is exactly what it sounds like—a simple catchall for those important reminders, papers, and documents that easily get lost or scattered. It's a daily reference for your tasks, and once you start using one, you'll wonder how you managed without it.

You can use a basic three-ring binder, a Moleskine notebook, a simple folder, or even an accordion-style expanding file. Use whatever works best for you and your organizational style. The important thing is to make it practical, easy to use, and something that serves *you*—not the other way around.

So once you have your notebook, what do you put in it? There's not a definitive list you must follow, because it's meant to serve as your daily tool. Simply fill it with what's important to you and your job. But to give you some ideas, here are the items I find most useful.

1. Daily Docket

A daily docket is a to-do list on steroids. I created this personalized form to house all my basic notes for one day. It includes my to-do list, the menu plan for the day, a simple appointment calendar, free space to jot down scribbles and notes, and even a spot to write down some inspirational quotes or thoughts to keep me motivated throughout the day. It's what works for me, and it's the space in my home management notebook I use most often.

Why It Works

There has been a lot written about the *best* way to manage your day at home, particularly with children. It's often suggested to create a specific timetable for the day, and then rotate weekly jobs set in stone on different days of the week. Writing out this schedule and putting it in a visible place lets you know what to do next.

This is a great idea in theory, but most of our lives are a lot more unpredictable. When I tried to make Thursdays my laundry day, or scheduled one-on-one time with my daughter at eleven o'clock Monday through Friday, I was trapped. I was trapped because *life* happened— one week I'd have an abnormally large amount of laundry, and trying to do it all in one day doomed me to failure because there just wasn't enough time for it. Time with my daughter would get pushed back because we really needed to run errands at eleven o'clock or she needed an earlier nap. Plus, when children are very young, their needs change almost monthly. If I were to create a rigid schedule that finally worked for me, a month later I'd need to throw it out and start all over because my kids' needs changed.

After a long time of searching for that "perfect" routine in my life at home, I felt like throwing any semblance of routine out the window. Nothing I tried had worked. But deep down, I knew a routine would help me. I love checking things off a list, plus I'm a visual learner, so it helps to see my day's plan.

What eventually evolved is now my daily docket, a marriage of scheduled routine and flexibility. It provides a skeleton on which I can hang my agenda, but it allows for wiggle room because I fill out a new sheet each day. So instead of a set routine on Mondays, I fill out a fresh sheet for that one day, using a simple weekly checklist as my resource. My week's main goal is to get my checklist done by the weekend, but I'm flexible as to when specifically I should do it.

How It Works

The night before, I take one of my daily dockets and fill it out for the next day. It helps if I use a pencil because things are unpredictable in our home, and flexibility is key.

I jot down that day's dinner plans, along with anything I need to do in advance to have dinner on the table on time—run to the store for bread, marinate the chicken in the morning, or get it all in the slow cooker by noon, for example. I list any appointments that have set times so that I can carve the rest of my day around those. I like listing my food choices for the day and ticking off how many glasses of water I'm drinking so that I can visually see how I'm physically taking care of myself. And in conjunction with my to-do list, I separately write out my most important things.

I limit my to-do list to ten things because I know I realistically can't check off more than that. I've actually almost *never* gotten all ten accomplished in one day. By keeping it short, I'm making success—finishing my list—more of a reality. If I remember additional things throughout the day, I jot them down in my notes section, probably to be added to tomorrow's list.

At first glance, my daily docket looks a lot more structured than it is, but I don't write out a timetable for every last thing I want to do that day. I only assign a time slot to those things I need to focus on at a specific time. I want to get work done on the computer during my kid's nap time, so I remind myself that computer work is a 2 P.M. job. I'd like to get breakfast on the table by eight, so I make a note of that. And most importantly for me, I want to get to bed by 10:30 P.M. Seeing it on paper reminds me that it's important.

Appendix C has a basic daily docket template for you to enlarge, photocopy, and use in your own home management notebook. You can also download a template for free by going to SimpleMom.net and clicking on *downloads*.

The Most Important Tasks

Mothers in particular are busy, and by default of the job description, they're multitaskers. There's no other way to do a load of laundry *and* pay bills *and* buy groceries *and* make dinner *and* spend quality time with our kids and spouses.

But still, the number one enemy of productivity in any adult's life—especially when she has very small children at home—is trying to do too much.

I have never accomplished everything I need to do in one day. This is the very reason why trying to do too much will set us up for failure. To put it bluntly, if we think we'll successfully check off a twenty-item to-do list within twenty-four hours, we're kidding ourselves.

Life happens. We want to organize our kids' clothes, but then our husbands will need help with such-and-such for a work project. We hope to get the weeding done, but our neighbor's mom just died, and it's really more important to bring our neighbor a meal (remember, relationships are more important than to-do lists). For my sanity, for my clarity, for my goal-oriented self, I've employed the concept of "most important tasks" (MITs).

It's not a new concept, and it's almost too simple to need explanation, but it's been revolutionary in my life. I make my to-do list on my daily docket, and then above this, I list my MITs.

My MITs are the top three things I want to accomplish that day. If nothing else gets done, I'd say my day was a success if I finish those three things. They usually focus on my job around the home, but they also sometimes focus on a personal habit I'm working on. For example, my MITs today are:

1. Wash, dry, fold, and put up one load of laundry
2. Sort and organize the kids' clothes
3. Exercise

The first task is purely home management—we've got to have clean clothes to wear. The second task is slightly longer term; as I look ahead to purging the clothes that no longer fit, I'll need to know what needs replacing. And the third task is important for my personal health, and by making it a high priority, I'll be more likely to accomplish it. It'll benefit both my family and me in the long run.

I'll focus on these tasks, knowing I've got much more to do than just these three. But now that I'm channeling my energy to only three items, I'll feel truly accomplished when they're done. And when I finish these tasks and move on to checking off other things on my day's to-do list, then that's an added bonus.

Please note that my MITs are already part of my to-do list. They're not separate entries—otherwise, they would just be additions to the to-do list. Using the example above, here's my day's complete to-do list:

1. Wash, dry, fold, and put away one load of laundry
2. Sort and organize the kids' clothes
3. Exercise
4. Finish organizing craft cabinet
5. Call Mom

6. Spend quality time as a family—maybe go on a picnic for dinner?
7. Gather receipts to update this month's budget
8. Declutter my desk
9. Work on my writing projects
10. Reply to e-mails

So in essence, my MITs are the three top things on my ten-item to-do list.

The daily docket is focused on productivity, but remember, that's not the only definition of a good day. I'm a list-maker, but I must be mindful not to worship my day's list. Life happens. When those three MITs don't happen, it's not the end of the world. I just wake up and start a new day.

2. Cleaning Checklist

To use my daily docket, I refer to my simple cleaning checklist. It provides me with a master plan of what I usually need to accomplish in a typical week. It helps to not have to remember on the fly what needs cleaning—I can just check my master list. It also keeps me accountable for those weekly tasks that I too easily slide under the rug.

Unlike my daily docket, I have only one master checklist printed, and I keep it in a clear sleeve in my home management notebook. Then I use a dry-erase marker to tick off the tasks I've completed throughout the week. At the start of a new week, I wipe it clean and start over. I rarely get everything checked off in a given week, but having a master list as a visual reminder really helps.

You can easily make yourself a master checklist based on what's most important in your family. Create it on the computer and print out multiple copies, or just hand write a simple list and slide it into a clear sleeve. Feel free to enlarge and copy the weekly checklist in appendix C. That list represents what's on my checklist, but there are no right or wrong tasks to include. Add to (or subtract from) this list as needed. Customize it so it works for you.

Under the "miscellaneous" category, I pencil in items as I remember them, and if I seem to be penciling in the same item week after week, I permanently add it to the list. I also have two short checklists under this longer weekly list. They are:

Basic Daily Cleaning
____   make the beds
____   wash and put away the dishes
____   wipe down the kitchen counters
____   pick up clutter
____   quickly sweep the living/dining area
____   quickly sweep the kitchen
____   file away paperwork

Monthly Organizing Tasks
____   organize the pantry
____   inventory our food supply
____   menu plan
____   write our monthly budget
____   organize the wardrobes

3. Monthly Calendars

I use Google Calendar for my personal day timer, and I usually just refer to it online to keep track of my appointments. I particularly like that I can have it remind me of events via e-mail or pop-up—very handy when I'm writing e-mails and I've lost track of time. But I also print the calendar several months at a time to keep handy when I'm not near my laptop and I want to jot something on the schedule. I also menu plan monthly, and I enter this on the online calendar. So when I print the calendar, I have a month's worth of dinner plans easily accessible in my notebook. If you'd rather stick to pen and paper, you can download simple monthly calendar pages for free by going to SimpleMom.net and then clicking on *downloads*.

4. Master Grocery List

I've written up my family's master grocery list in Excel, and it's a lifesaver. Having my usual purchases already printed out helps trigger my memory, and I've listed the food in order by aisle for my local store. When I'm shopping, I start at the top and wind my way through the store following the list. Organizing everything by the aisle cuts my shopping time in half.

I normally keep the current grocery list hanging in the kitchen so that anybody can mark what we need, but I also keep several fresh lists handy in my notebook. When we need a new list, I simply pull one out. I also have several blank pages of paper in this section for me to jot down menu and food ideas, which is especially handy when I'm browsing the Internet or leafing through my cookbooks.

5. Monthly Budget

I fill out my family's monthly zero-based budget online, and then I print a copy of this and keep it for handy reference in my notebook. We've used PearBudget.com for several years and have been very happy with the program and the service. It's simplicity at its finest and well worth the three dollar monthly fee.

I also write out our current financial goals and where we stand on reaching them, and house any other financial information that might prove relevant that month (bank statements, important receipts, and the like). My husband has a lot of work reimbursements for his job, and I also keep track of these here. I have a little plastic envelope where I keep all of his current month's receipts.

You'll find a simple monthly zero-based budget worksheet in appendix C.

6. Master Project List

My brain is flooded with little ideas throughout the day, and if I don't write them down within a few minutes, they leave and they don't return. I have a few blank sheets of paper in a section I call the master project list. I use these open space to jot down anything that comes to mind that I want to work on—for example, make slipcovers for the pillows, fix the bathroom towel bar, buy a specific book.

Having this free space in the notebook adds a nice combination of order and stream of consciousness to my thought process. I can doodle, outline, or list, and that freedom really helps me. Let this space reflect your thought process to make the most of it.

7. Work ideas

Similar to the above, I keep blank paper handy for jotting down work ideas. If I don't, they're gone, and frustration inevitably ensues.

8. Babysitter's Guide

Our kids are pretty easy to care for, but we want to keep current information handy when someone else watches our kids. We list our cell phone numbers, bedtime routines, what's off limits, and what to do in case of basic emergencies (like where we keep our first-aid kit). We even have instructions on how to turn on our TV and DVD player. You can enlarge and copy the master babysitter's guide in appendix C.

9. Things for the Kids

I jot down ideas or Web sites that come in handy for anything regarding my children. If I find an article online or in a magazine that's particularly relevant at the moment, I'll print it out and keep it here.

10. Gift Ideas

When my parents ask me what I want for my birthday, I usually can't think of anything at the moment. In this section, I jot down any gift ideas I have for my family, along with good gift ideas for us to give to others. We use a free online service called Wishpot.com to track gift ideas online, but this notebook space is helpful when I'm not at the computer and need to write an idea down before it disappears.

11. Personal Notes

This is where I write down fascinating quotes I come across, prayer requests, and anything else related to my personal life and my relationships. I also write down my goals and the habits I want to change. It helps me to see them in writing.

Putting It All Together and Making It Work for You

The trick is to have your home management notebook complete enough for it to be useful, but not so crammed full or overcomplicated that it's uninspiring and lackluster. This should be a valuable tool for home management. Design it so it works for you. Don't become enslaved by it.

Here are a few final tips to help you get the most enjoyment out of your home management notebook:

- The point of a notebook is to have all of your management tools in one place. Include what you need; leave out what you don't. If you find that after a while you never refer to a section in your notebook, take it out.
- Do what works for you. If you prefer to scribble with a pencil in a plain journal, then by all means, do that. You could even have it all online using your favorite tools in one location.
- It helps me if my notebook is aesthetically pleasing—I use it more when I like to look at it. Use scrapbook paper, magazine clippings, stickers, or whatever else strikes your fancy to personalize your notebook with your signature touch.
- Should your notebook not work for you at first, don't throw in the towel. Give it more time, change it up, or take a short break

and think about what might work better for you. We all manage our households differently. The goal is to do it well, simply, and without stress.

- Add a pocket, envelope, or folder to the notebook to hold any loose papers you need to keep with it. Or use paperclips to secure loose items and keep them from getting lost or scattered.

7 | Savor the Little Things

Rewards of Simple Living

"Enjoy the little things, for one
day you may look back and realize they were the big things."

–ROBERT BRAULT

This is when all the discussing and planning from the previous chapters finally comes together in a big-picture vision of the life you hope to create. There's something in most of us that cherishes the little things in life. You may have enjoyed an adventurous vacation or two during your childhood, but I'd wager a bet that most of your fond memories involve something little, something day-to-day, something commonplace: summer evenings chasing fireflies with your sister; the lingering hours spent engrossed in a book, oblivious to the world around you; drinking hot chocolate in front of the fireplace, while watching the snow flutter and flit outside the window.

Sounds Rockwellian, doesn't it? Perhaps those moments are a bit idealistic, but you probably *did* have a moment or two like that as a child, didn't you? What details do you remember of that exotic family vacation? Do you remember how much money it cost to enter a tourist attraction or what education you gained from the specific details of a historic site? Probably not, but you might remember sitting in the back-seat of a car, watching the world gallop by as your family road-tripped its way to a destination.

As human beings, we cherish the little things. Big events are grand, and if we're blessed enough to experience some, we should be grateful. But at the end of the day, what we all want and need—children and adults alike—is a full life, one dripping with meaning and richness.

That richness comes from savoring the everyday, from having enough time and sanity to notice the meaningful moments when they appear and enjoy them as they linger. The beauty of finding your purpose is that when you give it room to create a simpler life for your family, you'll have more time and leisure to enjoy these little things.

The problem is that most people don't have that time and sanity. They're too busy. Their lives are too crowded and complicated, as we discussed in Chapter 4. They'd like to get off the ride and reclaim some of those childhood memories in their adult life, but they're not sure what to cut or how to slow down. But the solution must go further than simply finding that commitment on the calendar to eliminate or tossing some of the clutter out of your house.

The underlying issue is misplaced priorities. To find a true solution, you must redefine your priorities as a family and solidify the purpose of your home. You recently spent time crafting your family's life purpose. What is the purpose of your home, the place where your family lives out much of its purpose? Is it to house a bunch of stuff? Or is it a haven in which you can savor life?

A Home That Embraces the Little Things

Can you imagine what it would be like to not *have* to spend hours a day folding clothes, picking up toys, and running errands? It just might be possible to enjoy moments watching your kiddos run through the sprinkler in the backyard or to take up that craft you long ago delighted in sans children.

When your home runs efficiently and when it's free of all but the essentials, *you* are more free to enjoy life. You still need to cook and clean, of course, but even those activities can be enjoyable when you're not stressed and panicked over them. They don't rule over you as a master. Those tasks are simply part of your day, along with the playing and the crafting.

In fact, the cooking and the cleaning can *be* your play and craft. You can learn skills you've always wanted to acquire, but have never had the time to learn because you were always too busy running on the hamster wheel of life because of your clutter. You can actually make your life the thing you want, instead of watching from the sidelines those lives you admire and want to emulate. Life is short. Make the most of it *now*. Don't spend precious hours dealing with the clutter in your life rather than experiencing those moments you crave.

Let your home serve as a tool for living holistically with your life's purpose. Don't let it compete. Align your living space with your values.

A Life Enjoyed

Here are a few things we're able to enjoy when our home is decluttered and efficiently organized.

Using Your Hands

You can create both treasures and necessities with your hands because you have the time these activities require. Sewing your children's clothes requires time and space. If you've always wanted to learn this craft, or if you know you already love to sew and you crave the time you need for it, then you've got to have a simple, streamlined home to accommodate this activity. The same goes for arts like knitting, painting, woodworking, and scrapbooking. Whatever craft is your cup of tea, your home should allow for the creativity you crave. Instead of wishing you didn't have so much stuff or dreaming of that additional room devoted to your craft, make your home work for you *now*. If, like me, you only have room for sewing on your dining room table, sacrifice other things in order to make sewing in this central part of the home an enjoyable process. Declutter until you find that storage space you need. Will a few extra vases, a bulky buffet, or a second set of dishes really make your life more meaningful? Probably not. But teaching your daughter to knit or making room for some tools for your husband to hone his woodworking hobby just might. We value life experiences. Things are just things.

Amanda Soule, blogger and author of *The Creative Family* and *Handmade Home*, recently told me, "The beautiful thing about the position so many of us are in—this day and age—is that we have so many choices about how we choose to spend our time, energy, and resources. Making things by hand does take a bit more time, surely, but if creating is something that brings you joy, it can add so many other things to our lives besides just the item's given purpose. Making things by hand nurtures ourselves, connects our families, and conserves both financial and environmental resources."

Crafting with our hands isn't the only thing we have to gain with a simple home. You can learn life skills, like changing your car's oil, painting your home's exterior, fixing your leaky faucet, mending a fallen hem, or replacing a missing button because you have the time to learn them. As a consumer culture, we've lost the artful appreciation of self-sufficiency. These days, we need only to drive to our neighborhood quick-stop oil change shop to service our vehicles. A leak-free faucet is only one pricey phone call away.

A few generations ago, men and women usually relied on practical know-how and neighborly help when something was broken or outdated. They repaired, mended, and breathed additional life into their material objects. They didn't immediately run out to a big-box home improvement store to replace a worn wheelbarrow with a brand-new one. They knew how to make something work.

I have no problem with luxuries from a gargantuan hardware store. It's wonderful that we can efficiently run our homes with today's technologies and inventions. But we are a throwaway culture, and we don't take the time or energy needed to teach ourselves how to help make an object last. We'd rather just go out and buy a new one.

Doing things yourself might cost you more time in the short run, but remaining an adolescent in your ability to self-preserve costs you money, added material waste, and pride in your ability to pass down those dying arts of homemaking and community service to your children. Don't let the skills of repair and crafting fade in your lifetime— make sure future generations know how to responsibly care for their items and how to create their own.

Cooking From Scratch

The birth of modern-day convenience food coincided with the dawn of dual working-parent families, increased efficiency from technological inventions, and more dexterous city planning. I don't need to hypoth esize the dangers of fast food and prepackaged chemicals disguised as real food because you've probably already heard them.

A home that nourishes life embraces the little moments and appreciates the rhythmic seasons of life, including the time necessary to cook real food from scratch. Scratch cooking does take time, to be sure. Heating up dinner from a box takes less effort than boiling real potatoes, assembling a fresh green salad with chopped seasonal vegetables, and sautéing chicken breasts in olive oil and garlic. It doesn't have to take too much time, however, with efficient menu planning and wisely planned trips to the grocery store and farmers' market.

The payoffs are astronomical—better health, good stewardship of our environment, and setting a good example for our children are just a few of the benefits. It also fosters an appreciation of the ebbs and flows of seasons because you'll be using fresh ingredients that are more readily available (and of higher quality) when they are in season. If you feel too busy to cook from scratch, then I argue that you're too busy, period. Reevaluate your priorities and commitments. If you want to live a healthy, long life and to pass the same luxury on to your children, then you *must* take the time to cook real food.

You can even grow your family's own food and store some of it during the off-season via canning and freezing. However, this endeavor requires time and space. Working in a simplified home will make this task a much more rewarding and less hectic process.

Entertaining and Socializing

When was the last time you invited family or friends over for dinner with only a few days' notice? A simple home invites an atmosphere of hospitality, where you can make casual, last-minute plans to have your neighbors over for iced tea. When basic upkeep takes just a few minutes a day, you don't need to stress when your son wants to invite his friend and his friend's mom over after baseball practice. When you take the time to declutter and purge your home of the unnecessary, you buy time for the future to enjoy your home and share it with others.

How Small Pleasures Connect With a Simple Home

When you own fewer things, those things retain a higher value to you. Having one high-quality skillet instead of five subpar ones means that you'll probably take better care of the one than if you had more than you needed. After you've sold all the DVDs that you don't watch, you're left with the ones you truly enjoy, which means you really love your movie collection. You are able to find the film you want with minimum effort, and when you return it to its case after watching, you're ensuring that you will enjoy it again.

When you own less, you take better care of the things you keep in your home because you've adhered to the mantra coined by the nineteenth century artist and designer William Morris: "Have nothing in your house that you do not know to be useful, or believe to be beautiful." You value your possessions. They don't own you, and you're free to enjoy them.

And when you have the time to craft items, you treat them as treasures. As Soule says, "I find that including so much handmade in our family life helps us to lead simpler, more mindful days together. When we make something versus buying it, we're aware of how much time and energy went into the production of it, which makes us more mindful of the purchases we *do* make. So it does slow us down, but in really wonderful ways, I believe."

Make your home a place where you *can* slow down. Don't just wish for it and watch with helplessness as your kids grow by the minute. Choose *now* to make your home a haven that can serve your family's desires and dreams, and don't waste any more time enslaving yourselves as its servant. Life is too short to miss out on the little things.

8 | A Home That Works

Create Your Family's Haven for a Simple Life

"Three rules of work: Out of
clutter find simplicity; from discord
find harmony; in the middle of
difficulty lies opportunity."

–ALBERT EINSTEIN

So far, we've discussed streamlining your family finances, gone through ways to keep your family calendar manageable, and created a home management notebook to help you efficiently run your home. Changing your habits in all of these areas is crucial for simplifying your life and living holistically with your life's purpose.

But if your *physical* world is still full of clutter, you're probably still stressed, overwhelmed, and busy with needless maintenance. Your living space needs to reflect how you want to live your life: at peace, with enough time and money for the things that matter, and without things that just don't matter. This chapter will set the stage for the cleaning and organizing you will do later in the book.

Creating a more peaceful living space doesn't happen overnight, nor does this tranquility remain forever unchanged once you've arrived at uncluttered nirvana. A peaceful home requires a change of attitude, a habit of regular maintenance, and a lifelong commitment to place higher priority on relationships and events than on things.

If you want to have a home that is easy to clean, easy to find things in, and easy to enjoy, then it will take work. And depending on your home's status right now, it might take some hard work.

But the good news is that it can be done. You are not a victim of clutter, and you do not have to give in to its stressors or believe that it will take too long or too much energy to overhaul all of your stuff. The lifestyle you want won't happen passively. It takes effort and intention to create that lifestyle and to create a home that embodies it. Choose *today* to make your home a haven for your entire family, one that allows each member to live at peace.

Opportunity Cost

In the economic world, "opportunity cost" means the cost of an alternative that must be forgone in order to pursue a certain action. Put another way, opportunity cost is the benefit you could have received by taking an alternative action. You have fifteen dollars, and you have a choice to buy either a shirt or a book. If you choose the shirt, the opportunity cost is the book; if you go with the book, then your opportunity cost is the shirt. When a young adult chooses to go to college for four years instead of entering the work force right away, she is forgoing an income (opportunity cost)—of course, with the hope that an earned degree will provide a higher income and therefore offset the income foregone during her college years.

Opportunity cost is just as important at home and in the family, and it should be a factor in our decision making. Every purchasing choice has a price tag. When you choose to buy something, what you are saying is that to you, the item is worth its asking price, and you are willing to part with that amount of money for the privilege of calling it your own. But you also pay a price when you choose *not* to buy something (your opportunity cost). You're choosing to live without that object, and the "cost" involved is the consequence of not owning it. It could be a deliberate choice—you don't like how the item fits you, let's say, so you leave it on the rack. Or it could be a forced choice—you don't have the money available to buy the item, so you have to learn to live without it (and credit cards are *never* a logical option in this scenario).

Consider this: When you choose to have something inside your house, what exactly is it you're choosing? You're choosing to own the item, yes, but you're also choosing the other, less noticeable price tags that follow. Whatever its size, you're choosing to lose empty square footage. You're choosing to part with money. Perhaps you're choosing a decorative look of "more" instead of "less" in your home. The opportunity costs involved are money in your pocket, less space in your home, and a more cluttered look.

None of these choices are necessarily bad. An item might very well be worth all of those things and more, so the opportunity cost is lower than the benefit of owning it. But there's still an often unseen opportunity cost—the price tag of not having it.

In other words, whether you are aware of it or not, you are making a choice to own and keep every item you have in your home. The important thing to ask yourself is: Is the choice to *have* the thing in your home worth missing the opportunity to *not* have it? Do you value owning the item more than you value the liquidity and open space you have without the item? If you value the item more, buy it or continue to keep it in your home. If you value the money and the space more, don't buy the item, or sell it if you already own it.

Let's say you splurge a few extra bucks to get a mattress that helps you sleep better. You've had back problems for some time, so while you were saving money by not buying a new mattress, you were paying a price by sacrificing your comfort and your sleep quality. When you buy the new mattress, you part with some money, but you gain something that is worth that price. You feel better and sleep better, so you're more refreshed, and therefore, more productive and healthier. For you, the money is worth it. The opportunity cost (a pain-free back and better sleep) is higher than the cost of ownership (the monetary cost of the mattress), so the expense is justified.

Let's do one more example. You have a china collection that you've had since your wedding. You've used it twice in ten years, but you hold on to it because it's expensive. Understandable. But there's still a price to keeping it in your home, and it just might be higher than the price of letting it go. You're not only missing out on some decent money you could get by selling the china, but you're also paying for less room in your cabinets, more dishes to pack as you move, more things to dust, more areas off-limits for your kids. More clutter. More stuff. The china *could* be worth those things, but it might not be worth them.

You're not a victim. You allow each item in your home to be there. Do you love it all? Do you find it useful or beautiful?

The surprising effect of getting rid of the things that you don't love is that you grow deeper in love with the things you choose to keep. Your kids love every toy they own. You'd gladly wear every pair of jeans in your closet. You like all the music in your CD collection. Simplifying is not parting with love. It's gaining it.

Diving in Headfirst

Your home didn't magically become cluttered and disheveled on its own, and neither will it magically organize itself. As I mentioned before, simple living requires work. It won't be easy to overhaul your home, but it will be worth it. It involves physical work, yes, but it's also a mental and emotional workout.

You'll need to think about your possessions differently, and you'll need to change your habit of associating *more* with *better*. It might even become emotional for you.

The best way to tackle this kind of hard work is by taking one bite at a time—just like eating an elephant. You can't expect to turn your home upside down in one afternoon and then flip it right-side up, looking spic and span in time for dinner. It will take multiple hands and multiple days. Many hands make light work; slow and steady wins the race. You get the idea.

Even if you're fired up about tossing all the clutter and creating a simpler home, you might be surprised at how difficult it will be to decide whether to sell your grandmother's jewelry that you inherited but never wear. Sometimes it's worth the extra space. Sometimes it's not. Only you can make that decision.

The first part of this book has hung some nails in the wall. The next portion of this book will give you practical tips you can hang on those nails, creating that space for the holistic life you crave. And because this is a lifelong journey, not a quick fix, we're only starting with a ten-day jump start.

I propose to you that in ten days, you can surprise yourself with a major home overhaul that will jump you out of the starting gate and give you a huge head start. With a three-step process of decluttering, organizing, and cleaning, you can help your home look much more congruent with your family's purpose. And because simple living is *living holistically with your life's purpose*, you will be so much closer to living a simple life.

It's not magic, it's work. It requires persistence, a willing attitude, and probably a little dirt and sweat. You'll need to carve out deliberate time on the calendar, and the more family members who can get involved, the better.

Visualizing Your Goals

It's time to use your family purpose statement again. What is your family about? What goals do you share? How can you best use your gifts? Don't underestimate the power of a living space congruent with your family culture. If you share life in a home that's holistically aligned with your family's purpose, then it'll be so much easier to be yourself, to feel at home, and to reach your goals.

Sometimes it's easy for you to *create* a family purpose statement, but you're at a loss on what that purpose statement looks like within your four walls. What exactly does it mean to have a holistically congruent living space? If your family values nature and the outdoors, does that mean you should knock out the walls and live out in the open? Of course not. But maybe it means you create a type of family space in your backyard and move your television out of the living room and into an office. That way, you're better able to enjoy your plot of soil out back, and you're less tempted to veg in front of the TV, merely *wishing* you all spent time together outside.

It will look different for each family because each family has its own set of values and its own purpose statement. For some, a backyard might not be that important, so they'd rather create a living space that makes it easier to entertain. They'd make more of a priority to have adequate seating, an open furniture arrangement, and a kitchen that works well for large feasts. They're fine with a simple patch of grass that needs an occasional mow.

Look at your family purpose statement and review your priorities. Make a mental picture of how this statement would look fleshed out within your four walls. Write down some words you want to describe the overall feel of your home. After someone spends time in your home, what would you like them to say about it?

Touring Your Home

Using your purpose statement, walk through each room of your house together as a family and talk about how that room would function in order to reflect your purpose. Don't visualize your dream home—no "I need granite countertops in order to have company over for dinner," or "we really need a Jacuzzi tub in order to make our master bathroom be a place of comfort and security." This is the stuff that could reasonably happen *now*, without major additions or remodeling.

If creativity is of high value for your family, then it makes sense to have a communal work space in order to create. Perhaps that means having an art supply cabinet in the playroom or musical instruments available in the living room.

If the general vibe you want in your home is *peace*, then it's best not to have too much clutter, to keep the TV and DVDs behind closed doors, to make it easy to play music, and perhaps to keep sweet-smelling candles within arm's reach.

You'll have more time to decide what each room's purpose is as you work through the ten-day jump start. But for now, as you tour your home, answer these questions about each room:

- What is the ideal purpose of this room? (Hint: There could be more than one purpose, such as the dining room serving both as a place to eat family meals *and* as the main learning quarters for your homeschool.)

- Who uses this room? Is it satisfying to them?
- Who doesn't use this room? Do they currently have belongings in this room that need to be transported elsewhere?
- In what ways will the ideal purpose of this room adequately reflect your family purpose statement?

Write your thoughts down and keep them with you. You'll need them soon.

Once you've overviewed your home and established a need for it to work congruently with your family purpose statement, it's time to roll up your sleeves and take some action.

Making the Most of What You've Got

Your current home may not be your ideal living quarters. Perhaps you're currently renting an apartment while you save up for a solid down payment. Maybe you live in an older home that needs a lot of sweat equity. Or maybe you bit off more than you can chew, and now your home feels a bit too big and overdone for how you want to live your life. There are so many ways your house could feel short of perfection. In fact, even if you custom built your dream home, it probably wouldn't take long to discover you wish you had an outlet on this wall instead of on that wall.

You can't wait to move into the "perfect" home to declutter and organize. You'll be waiting a long time because the perfect home doesn't really exist. You may eventually move into the perfect-for-*you* home, but don't wait for that elusive day to create the home you truly want. Choose *now* to make your current living space work to the best of its ability.

When to Change Living Spaces

There are times, however, when your family just might need to move. It's a big deal, I realize, and it's not a process that can happen overnight. But a minority of people might truly need to reconsider the viability of their family's current residence. Here are a few scenarios in which this might be the case.

1. You Have More Mortgage Than Money

A house that is too expensive is not ideal for anybody. You're robbing your family of joy, less stress, more opportunities, and perhaps even a more secure future when you're paying for more home than you can afford. Do what you can to refinance your mortgage, but if the numbers just don't work, then it's time to look things square in the face and change the situation. Even if you're upside down financially, it's better to trade a major debt for a smaller one and live in a home that allows you to sleep without stress.

2. It's Unlivable

Perhaps your home is incredibly old, and while it might have potential, it may take too much time, money, and energy to make it livable. You have the vision to make it a home, but maybe you bit off more than you can chew. Does it align with your family's purpose statement? Then great. But if repairing a difficult home in order to simply make it livable takes you away from living in the now and fleshing out your purpose, then it, too, is robbing your family of joy. Think long-term, of course, but it might be a better idea to hand over your fixer-upper to someone who can finish the job.

3. It Truly Doesn't Line Up With Your Family Purpose Statement

Most of the time, you can make your home work for your family. A small kitchen can be accommodated, and children can share a bedroom much more confidently than the world would lead you to believe. But there are times when the very bones and location of a home simply don't work for your family's purpose, and there's no way it will.

Are you in an urban high-rise apartment, and you've decided that it's a priority (more than just a *desire*) to live among nature, with green space outdoors for your kids to freely explore? There's not much you can do to grow a yard on an apartment balcony, no matter how hard you try.

But most of the time, you can make your current home work for you now. Be creative, and see what you can do to find workable solutions to live life holistically with your family purpose statement, no matter what sort of home you have.

Plant a Stake in the Ground

Creating a family living space that falls in line with your values will make it so much easier to flesh out your values in real life. Have you ever felt like your home doesn't quite "fit" your family's lifestyle, or that perhaps it looks more like someone else's residence? Or are there times when you're going along, living life, and you stop for just a moment and wonder *why* you're doing something? Perhaps you're stuck in traffic, taxiing one kid to soccer practice after picking up another kid from gymnastics, on your way to a fast-food drive-thru, and you just *know* something doesn't sit right with you. Then you come to your house and can't understand for the life of you why you financed furniture you don't really love and keep clutter that has no home. This isn't how you want to live your life. This isn't your family's ideal life.

Make a choice to live *your* life, full of your values and priorities, now. Put a stake in the ground as an ebenezer of remembrance that today, you are choosing to say *no* to unrealistic cultural expectations, and *yes* to the best life for your family.

I submit to you that one of the best ebenezers for your decision to live a simpler life is a purposeful, family-wide overhaul of the home. Write a date on the calendar *today* to start this ten-day process. And make it soon.

In the midst of the sweat and the exhaustion, you'll feel invigorated and renewed. You'll scan your home and feel like it's a few steps closer to being a workable, livable dwelling that makes sense to your family. If simple living means living holistically with your life's purpose, then it only makes sense to make your living space a place that aligns with and reflects your purpose.

Ready to begin? Good.

PART TWO

Ten Days to a Simpler, More Organized Home

DAY 1:

A Fresh Start, a New Direction

"Simplicity, simplicity, simplicity!
I say let your affairs be as two or
three, and not half a hundred or
a thousand."

—HENRY DAVID THOREAU

It's here—the beginning of your fresh start. For the next ten days, we are going to focus on one area of your home per day, working by a methodical process of decluttering, cleaning, and organizing. I can't promise it won't be tiring or difficult. But it will be worth it. Armed with your new purpose statement fresh in your mind and with plenty of encouragement to simplify your life, this fresh start will be a stake in the ground for a new lifestyle. Just think—in ten days or so, your home will better reflect who you are as a family. It won't be perfect, and it won't be completed for all time. But you *will* be much further ahead toward creating a space that fosters growth, unity, and freedom to express your family's purpose with enthusiasm.

The Game Plan

Today, you're going to move quickly through every room in your home. You'll make decisions about all the easy stuff—things you *know* you don't want around anymore. Let's get rid of it. You'll also start getting ready for the yard sale your family will have in the next two months.

What You'll Need:

- ☐ Two large boxes labeled "give" and "sell," or more, if you think you might need them
- ☐ One box labeled "maybe"
- ☐ A garbage can
- ☐ Price tags and a marker for a yard sale you'll have in the next two months
- ☐ A ruthless spirit

First, toss any visible trash into the garbage can—wrappers, tiny crayon bits, and the like. Go through the entire living space of your home. Move quickly, though—don't start digging underneath your couch cushions. We'll get to that. If you know items are recyclable, take the time to toss them in the right receptacle. Piles of paper, magazines, and newspapers should all skip the trash can for the recycle bin.

This shouldn't take you too long. If you're spending a lot of time on this task, then you're being too methodical. Tossing all trash should be a quick and focused activity. Don't get distracted into organizing and sorting, and don't overanalyze the value of your old, unread newspapers. They're not worth reading if they're more than two days old—start fresh with tomorrow's paper. Just toss them. You'll feel better.

Once you've done this, start in one corner of your home and move out, eyeing each item. As you do this, think about William Morris's quote: "Have nothing in your house that you do not know to be useful, or believe to be beautiful."

Calculate every item's value by asking yourself two questions:

1. Is this thing useful to me (us)?

2. Is this thing beautiful to me (us)?

If you answer *no* to both of these questions, toss it in either the give or the sell box. It might be beautiful to another family, or they might find the perfect use for it—but for you and your family, it is taking up space. It is cluttering your home physically and visually, and this has a direct impact on your peace of mind, your sanity, and your joy at home. Is this item truly worth all of those things? If so, then keep it. But if it isn't positively contributing toward making your home a haven, the thing is just that—a thing. Get rid of it.

Scan each room in your home and repeat this with all the visible stuff, over and over. This should be a quick project. If you have to stop and think through an item's value, and you can't decide within a few minutes, move on. You'll have a chance to reevaluate later.

Please note that I'm talking about the obvious stuff—now isn't the time to sort through your coat closet or your teenage son's first-grade artwork or any drawers in the room. This is about the stuff that really doesn't take any effort to find. This is the magazine collection in the bathroom, the trinkets on the end tables, and the knickknacks on your dresser—anything that's visible as soon as you enter the room.

Today's Items to Deal With Are:
- Coupons, notes, and drawings hanging on the fridge
- The needless figurines cluttering your surfaces
- Pennies and nickels scattered throughout the house in containers
- Stacks of old newspapers and magazines
- Unloved throw pillows and blankets scattered about

Today's Items Not to Worry About Are:
- Your wedding dress
- The filing cabinet
- Your junk drawer
- Holiday decorations stored up in your attic
- Books and other items tucked away on your shelves
We'll get to all of these later.

In other words, today's chore is a big one, but it's meant to be breezy and swift, not heart-wrenching and difficult. This is about the stuff you've always thought shouldn't be in your home, but you never really took the time to deal with it. Today's the day to take care of it. By the end of your work, you should be able to look around your home and not see anything you don't want. And, believe it or not, at the end of these ten days, there's a chance you'll even change your mind about some of those things that, right now, you can't imagine living without.

Don't forget about the other people in your family. In fact, get them to help you make decisions because what's beautiful to one person may not be to another. You might be annoyed by your son's rock collection, your daughter's My Little Ponies, or your husband's T-shirts from college, but these people you love may hold a value to these things you can't even imagine. Don't use this as an excuse to keep things—if you know it's not loved, then do the deed and get rid of it. But if you're not sure, either get them to help or make piles of stuff belonging to each person and ask each family member to make decisions about his or her own things.

tip If you're hemming and hawing over an item, create a new box labeled "maybe" and write today's date on it. Put the item in there and store it in your garage or closet. Put a note on your calendar to check the box three months from today's date. Access the box as needed, but if, after three months, you're seeing those items for the first time (and they're not obviously seasonal), you don't need them. Looks like you have your answer.

The Dreaded Yard Sale

While you sweep through your home, arm yourself with stickers or masking tape and a marker, and price the items before moving them to the "sell" box. Pricing things now means not having to deal with a motherload of decision making later, and this will be the last time you'll have to see the things until the yard sale.

If you've kept an item in hopes that it's a collectible, use the Internet to find its value. Each category of collectible has seasons of highs and lows, so if you checked an item within the past year, check it again. EBay is a useful tool to find an item's going rate, and if the value looks somewhat promising, it might be worth it to post it and sell online. But if the value isn't worth the effort to pack and ship the item, then either post the thing on Craigslist or add it to your growing yard sale inventory.

Whatever you do, *don't* keep it with the hope of its value rising. It won't rise enough to be worth the rent in your home. Get rid of it. Get rid of it *now*.

Yard sales get a bum rap, and possibly with due cause. They're a lot of work, sometimes the profit doesn't feel worth the effort, and you have to get up at the crack of dawn on the weekends. But I want to argue the point that having a yard sale works psychologically to your advantage, and that the added benefit is extra change in your pocket.

I want you to schedule a yard sale sometime in the next two months—don't wait any longer, or else your "stuff" will seep back into your home, or you'll get used to the items dotting your garage's landscape. You can wait an extra month or so *only* if you're waiting on a preplanned neighborhood yard sale weekend or if you plan to participate in a larger gathering, such as a church sale.

Here are the reasons you need to take the time and effort required for a yard sale:

1. You'll Remember the Pain and Be Less Apt to Collect More Clutter

Much like the psychology behind making a child pay with chores for the broken window shattered by his baseball, forcing yourself to collect all of those things you don't need and sell them from your yard will hopefully deter you from needing to go through this effort again. If a weekend's devotion to selling your wares wipes you out, why go through it again? Perhaps you'll stop inviting needless clutter into your home in the first place.

2. It's a Great Way to See All the Stuff You Don't Want in One Place

When you leave clutter scattered about 2,000 square feet, it may not seem like much. But when you cram it all into your driveway, you'll be able to see the superfluous stuff you've been living with. It's psychologically humbling.

3. It's a Family Affair, Teaching Your Kids the Value—or Lack of Value—of Certain Items

Hopefully you'll get your kids involved. When you do, you'll give them a visual reminder that *things* cost money, and that the trade-off for owning needless stuff is more money for other things. Plus, it can be a good bonding experience and a lesson in money management, teamwork, and the importance of a good work ethic. Have your kids negotiate the prices of their toys and clothes. Let the smaller ones bag the sold items. And do what you can to lead the family with a good-hearted attitude.

4. You'll Get Extra Cash

You'll probably be rewarded with more money than you think. Three hundred dollars is a hefty chunk of bills, a whole lot of groceries, or several months of gasoline. Plus, there's the reward of getting rid of your things, one at a time, and returning through your front door with a more decluttered house.

The date of our yard sale is _____ _____ _____ .

If You're Feeling Emotional About Your Things

Sometimes it's natural to tie emotions with an object—your child's outfit she wore home from the hospital, for example, reminds you of how tiny she was and how fast time flies. But sometimes, we associate sentiment with an object because we think it holds a memory, when in reality, it's just another thing.

Does that figurine of a turtle made out of seashells remind you of your vacation to Key West? *Really?* Or can you remember your trip just as well without it? Are your memories in any way associated with that knickknack, or is it merely coincidental that you bought the thing on the same trip you enjoyed with your husband and kids? Get rid of the things that are just things—they're not useful, and you really don't find them that beautiful. By tossing them, you're not tossing the fun memories, nor are you saying that time with your family holds no meaning.

You have permission to keep the valid memories in your life and to toss the mere object you've associated with them. Your memories will remain, even if the objects are removed.

The next few steps are to overhaul the living room and kitchen, so get some rest and plan easy meals for the next few days.

 ## reflection questions

- Which items are you feeling emotional about? Jot down a few memories in your journal, or perhaps take a photo of the item before moving it to the sell box.

- As you look around your home, how do you feel now that the trash is gone and your needless items are prepped for selling or donating?

A Clean-Sweep Checklist:

Toss out the trash in these rooms:

- ☐ _____
- ☐ _____
- ☐ _____
- ☐ _____
- ☐ _____
- ☐ _____
- ☐ _____
- ☐ _____
- ☐ _____
- ☐ _____

Find things to sell and/or give away from these rooms:

- ☐ _____
- ☐ _____
- ☐ _____
- ☐ _____
- ☐ _____
- ☐ _____
- ☐ _____
- ☐ _____
- ☐ _____
- ☐ _____

10 | The Living Room

"The living room should be a
place where we feel totally at
ease—[a] temple of the soul."

–TERENCE CONRAN

The living room (or family room or den) is often the heart of the home. It's one of the few places where everyone in the family spends time, so it should be welcoming and appealing to all of your family members. It

What You'll Need:

CLEANERS

- ☐ Dish or laundry soap if the weather is warm*
- ☐ Rubbing alcohol
- ☐ Glass cleaner*
- ☐ Carpet and upholstery cleaner or some other mild soap*
- ☐ Vinegar
- ☐ Essential oils (optional)—my favorites are tea tree, lavender, and orange
- ☐ Mineral spirits (optional)
- ☐ Furniture polish* (optional)
- ☐ Woolite (optional)
- ☐ Baking soda (optional)

TOOLS

- ☐ Dust cloth, preferably microfiber
- ☐ Cleaning cloth, for upholstery

- ☐ Vacuum
- ☐ Hose attachment for the vacuum
- ☐ Wrapping paper tube or paper towel tube (if you don't have a vacuum attachment)
- ☐ Rubber gloves and an old sock if the weather is cool
- ☐ Cotton balls
- ☐ Old newspaper
- ☐ Broom
- ☐ Dustpan
- ☐ Mop
- ☐ Mop bucket
- ☐ New air-conditioning filters (optional)
- ☐ Your give and sell boxes
- ☐ Price tags and marker

* Homemade recipes for these cleaners are found in appendix A.

doesn't need to be magazine worthy, but it should be clutter free. As the central stomping ground for the family, you want people to *enjoy* being here. Clutter breeds stress, and if you let stuff take over this space, it'll ward off people. *People* are what make a home what it is—a haven for your family. Things should not take priority over relationships.

A simple home with a central gathering spot is an excellent breeding ground for a simple family life. The living room should be an essential part of your home.

The Game Plan

For the next two days, you'll be parked in the living room, family room, den, or whatever you call the central area in which you live the most. This area might include more than one room for you. You're going to declutter in a little more detail than yesterday, clean, and then organize all the items that will remain in these rooms. For motivation and inspiration, play some music and light a sweet-smelling candle or some incense. I also recommend displaying your family purpose statement; you might need a reminder of what you're about when it gets tough to make decisions.

What's the Purpose of Your Living Room?

As a family, decide what purpose you want this room to serve. What do you do here? Do you read? Play games? Watch movies? Probably. Make sure there's room for these activities. Today and tomorrow, remove the items that belong in another room, get rid of the things that aren't useful or beautiful, and clean and rearrange so that this space is a haven for the entire family. It'll be work, but it's worth it.

Remember that mindless TV watching is a horrendous time-sucker. Do you want all of your furniture to point at it, as though it's an altar of worship? Think about your family purpose statement—what is one of your main purposes as a family? Perhaps the showcase of this room should be your family library, or perhaps the fireplace, which would embody a spirit of hospitality or good conversation. I'm not saying the television shouldn't be in the living room, but if it is, don't by default assume that it must be the focal point. It will be easier to cut back on TV time if your furniture doesn't bow in adoration in its general direction.

Declutter

Remove everything but furniture, rugs, and curtains, and put it all in one central, roomy location. This would be the dining room table in my home, but if you're really short on space, consider your backyard. Lay down a tarp to protect items from grass and dirt, and to create a boundary for this staging ground. Take everything off of your coffee table, end tables, and media cabinet. If you have any baskets holding blankets or magazines, bring them, too. If your movies and games are stored behind cabinet doors, go ahead and empty those cabinets and put the things in your designated location. Even take books off the bookshelves and stack them in your designated location. Don't forget your "meta-stuff"—the stuff that holds your stuff. Baskets, boxes, drawer dividers, buckets, and tins—these are all examples of meta-stuff. You should now be left with wall hangings, furniture, and rugs.

Clean

Now that the room is emptied, it's much easier to clean. Work from the top down, so that dust and dirt travels south and you're not working against gravity.

Loosen any cobwebs from the corners of your walls. Dust the crown molding with a microfiber cloth, clean off your ceiling fan blades, and get the tops of your furniture, going from tallest to shortest. Also dust your furniture's shelves and the insides of the cabinets. Allow time for the dust to settle to the floor.

tip If you plan to live your normal life while working on this space, it might take more than two days. You have a few options about how to divide up the work. You want to make sure you don't go to bed with the place so disarrayed that you're discouraged and give up. It's important for your sanity to take bites, instead of devouring the entire elephant; allow plenty of time for clean-up after each day.

If these tasks involve more than one room, an obvious solution would be to devote one room per day. If your living area is one larger space, then declutter a bit at a time, cleaning and organizing one area before moving on to the next one. For example, just tackle your media cabinet first—remove the contents, clean, and replace what you're keeping, and then take the books off your bookshelf and do the same. Keep going until you cover each area of the room.

Resist the temptation to use store-bought furniture polish. According to Rachel Meeks at SmallNotebook.org, commercial-brand polishes "advertise that they leave a shine with no wax buildup, and that's true. The problem is that instead of wax, they contain petroleum derivatives, which leave a thin, oily residue on your furniture. If furniture has residue left from these products, then dusting with a plain damp cloth won't be very effective." Rachel suggests using mineral spirits (also called "white spirit" outside of North America), which you can buy at a hardware store. Don't worry about the mineral spirits harming the wood—it's a very mild solvent, recommended by many well-known home mavens, Martha Stewart being one. It will cut through the residue and remove the oil. After you clean the surfaces with mineral spirits, you should be able to use a simple damp rag for dusting all of your furniture. You'll never need to use commercial polishes again. If you truly feel like you must use polish, try using the homemade recipe found in appendix A.

Clean out your air-conditioning vents. If they're really bad, you might want to call a professional cleaning service, but if they're simply covered in dust, you can do it yourself. Unscrew the cover to the vent, and using a hose attachment on your vacuum, suck out the dust bunnies. If your hose-type vacuum doesn't have a narrow-end attachment, you can make one with an old cardboard tube from paper towels or gift wrap. Just squash the end down. Clean off the vent cover, and if it's bad, scrub it using soap and water. Dry the cover and screw it back on. Now's also a good time to change your filters, if it's been a while.

Clean your blinds, some of the worst dust traps in your home. If it's nice and sunny, put your blinds in the bathtub with hot water and a bit of dish or laundry soap. Let them soak there until the water is cool, and then bring them outside to dry—either hang them on a clothesline, or spread them out on a clean, dry surface, such as a patio. If the weather is inclement and you need to leave your blinds inside, leave them hanging on the windows. Wear a rubber glove and slide an old sock on top. Then dip your covered hand in rubbing alcohol and wipe all the blind's surfaces with your hand.

Clean your windows using glass cleaner and newspaper. I love the homemade recipe that can be found in appendix A, and adding orange essential oil gives it a wonderful, fresh, clean aroma.

Spot clean your upholstered furniture. Mix a couple capfuls of Woolite (or some other mild soap) in cool water, or make the homemade carpet and upholstery cleaner recipe found in appendix A. Dip and wring out a clean cloth so that it's barely damp. Carefully wipe off the fabric. Make sure all surfaces have the ability to air dry, and don't put cushions back until they're completely dry. You really don't need to soak the furniture, so it's vital not to use too much cleaner. If your furniture feels wet to the touch, you've used too much.

Wash your decorative pillows, throw blankets, and curtains with soap and water, if you're able (either by hand or in the machine). My favorite mild fabric cleaner is using soapnuts in the machine, or making a batch of homemade "soapnut soak" and washing by hand. Check the resources section for my favorite soapnut shop. If you don't have a natural, mild fabric cleaner on hand, then spot clean these items using the same method you used for your upholstered furniture.

You can sterilize surfaces using rubbing alcohol applied with a cotton ball. The living room checklist at the end of this chapter will help you remember these oft-forgotten places.

Clean your area rugs. First, sweep the rugs to loosen any dirt and to help the nap stand on end. Then use some homemade carpet and upholstery cleaner (recipe in appendix A) to spot treat any stains. If you've got stubborn, deep stains, try using the homemade heavy-duty carpet cleaner. Rub the paste into the stains and leave it for a few hours. When you're done removing the stains, finish off the rugs by vacuuming. Don't vacuum any fringe—this will pull on the threads and cause them to loosen and fray.

Treat carpet stains with the same method you used on your rugs. When the carpet is dry, vacuum it thoroughly. To neutralize any smells, sprinkle some baking soda and let it sit an hour before vacuuming.

Mop your floors with equal parts vinegar and hot water. If you'd like to add a scent, try a few drops of essential oil; as always, I think orange is one of the best smells for the home because it works in every season. It smells light and fresh in the spring and summer; cozy and festive in the autumn and winter holiday months.

Organize

Remember your things waiting for you in your designated location? It's time to put them back. Whoa—not so fast. It's time to put them back *if* they truly belong in the living room. If they make more sense in another room, put them there. And if you've grown to love this minimalist look in the living room and you feel like you can part with some stuff, that's even better. Put items in your give or sell boxes, and don't forget to price the things you want to sell. You've got a yard sale on the calendar, so add more to your pile of things for sale.

future project

If you've got sturdy-but-ugly cardboard boxes, you can cover them with fabric, wrapping paper, wallpaper, or scrapbook paper. Use a decoupage glue like Mod Podge, or make your own with three parts white glue to one part warm water. Mix thoroughly.

Remember, you care about living simply, or you wouldn't be reading this book and working through the mental and physical process of decluttering. Don't disappoint yourself by keeping too much stuff in the end. Every time you pick up one of the objects, ask yourself, "Is this useful or beautiful to anyone in the family?" If not, then it doesn't deserve residence in your home. Someone else may have a use for it, or another person may find it beautiful. Let them give this item a place of honor in their home. Make your life simpler *right now* by giving valuable real estate to only those items you love. You won't miss the other things.

After you've reassigned places for things that don't belong in the living room, get your meta-stuff—your baskets, your boxes, your trays. Are they in good shape? Do they work well? Do you like them? If so, great. Keep using them. Put things back in your meta-stuff, and place them where you're most likely to use them. If you'd most likely browse through your current magazines in your overstuffed chair, then your magazine basket belongs next to that chair.

If you have a shortage of meta-stuff, think outside the box (no pun intended) before grabbing your keys and heading to the store. Simple living is all about living well with less, putting the spotlight in your home on your life's purpose instead of showcasing the mere *stuff*. Do you have storage solutions that can be repurposed? If the cardboard box is going behind closed doors anyway, I wouldn't worry about beautify-ing it, at least for now—you've got more important things to do for the next few days, and that can always wait for a craft night. Jars, old pails, crates, and bags can all make great creative storage. Take care not to go overboard with eclecticism; otherwise, your living room might look like a dorm room. But flex your creative muscles—organizing doesn't have to cost a fortune.

If you have a lot of CDs or DVDs, consider buying a book that holds discs. There are some fabulous-looking disc holders that would look great on a shelf, and they don't cost a fortune.

If you can get this all done in one day, congratulate yourself, and either move on to Day Four, or take Day Three off. If you need to con-tinue in this area tomorrow, that's perfectly fine, too.

tip An eco-friendly and one-of-a-kind storage solution is to repurpose items like jars, crates, suitcases, vintage lockers, and bicycle baskets. Check your local flea markets, antique shops, Craigslist, or eBay for creative inspiration.

Step Back and Evaluate

What look do you like? Do you enjoy the kick-back-your-feet feel of a rumpled cottage, and to you, does an end table look unfinished when it's empty? Display your favorite items, just make sure you can answer yes to our two important questions:

1. Is it useful to you (us)?
2. Is it beautiful to you (us)?

If you prefer a more streamlined, minimalist look, then your work was probably halfway done before you returned your items. Really edit yourself—take a day before putting stuff back. If you wake up and the empty coffee table is a sight for sore eyes, you know your work is done.

If you don't know what look you like, go through magazines and Web sites, look at pictures, and bookmark looks you find appealing. It doesn't matter how you label your look—in fact, I like certain aspects of both the shabby-chic look and the sleek, modern look. Find some inspiration, and note specifically what it is that you like about the look.

 reflection questions

What is the main purpose of your living room? How does this central room help further your goals represented in your family purpose statement? What can you do to make it more of a haven for each family member? Do you feel like it reflects a simple life?

Your living room is probably the most used space in your home. You've got more work to do, but congrats—you just completed a big chunk of it.

Living Room Checklist:

DECLUTTER
- [ ] Bookshelves
- [ ] Coffee table
- [ ] End tables
- [ ] Media cabinet

CLEAN
- [ ] Dust all surfaces
- [ ] Clean air conditioner vents
- [ ] Change air conditioner filter
- [ ] Clean blinds
- [ ] Spot clean upholstered furniture
- [ ] Wash or spot clean pillows, throws, and curtains
- [ ] Dust art and wall hangings
- [ ] Sweep area rugs
- [ ] Clean floor and/or carpet

- [ ] Dust lampshades
- [ ] Dust ceiling fan blades
- [ ] Dust baseboards
- [ ] Dust shelves

DISINFECT
- [ ] All tabletops
- [ ] Table legs
- [ ] Cabinet doors
- [ ] Switch plates
- [ ] Door handles

ORGANIZE
- [ ] Books
- [ ] Magazines
- [ ] DVDs
- [ ] CDs
- [ ] Games

11 | The Kitchen

"The ability to simplify means to
eliminate the unnecessary so that
the necessary may speak."

–HANS HOFMANN

The kitchen can either be the most useful room in the house, or it can be the biggest clutter trap with a mishmash of purposes. As a veritable nucleus, a kitchen often serves as much more than the place to cook food—sometimes we eat, pay bills, hang out, keep track of the family

What You'll Need:

CLEANERS
- [ ] All-purpose cleaner*
- [ ] Liquid dish soap
- [ ] Glass cleaner*
- [ ] Oven cleaner*
- [ ] Rubbing alcohol
- [ ] Baking soda
- [ ] Lemon
- [ ] Essential oils (optional)
- [ ] Vinegar (optional)

TOOLS
- [ ] Sponge
- [ ] Scouring pad (depending on your surfaces)
- [ ] Toothbrush for cleaning
- [ ] Cleaning rag
- [ ] Vacuum
- [ ] Hose attachment for vacuum
- [ ] Wrapping paper tube or paper towel tube (if you don't have a vacuum attachment)
- [ ] Scraper, such as a spatula or an old credit card
- [ ] Cotton balls
- [ ] Broom
- [ ] Dustpan
- [ ] Mop
- [ ] Mop bucket
- [ ] Shelf-lining paper (optional)
- [ ] Paper and pen
- [ ] Newspaper
- [ ] Your give and sell boxes
- [ ] Price tags and a marker

* Homemade recipes for these cleaners are found in appendix A.

calendar, display artwork and photos, and toss the mail in the kitchen. This is all fine—if you're truly able to accomplish what you need to do in the kitchen. Are you able to cook without emptying all the cabinets to look for a tool? Can you organize your family's agenda with minimal paper clutter filling your counter spaces? If not, then it's time to make it happen. Make your kitchen work for your family.

The Game Plan

Small or big, the kitchen contains a lot of stuff. It's a big job, so we're going to stay here another two days.

What's the Purpose of Your Kitchen?

What happens in this space? The obvious function is cooking, but does the room serve this function well? Look around and see if your kitchen's arrangement is logical. It might seem obvious, but utensils you need for stovetop cooking need to be by the stove, and silverware and drinking glasses should be in a place where most of the family can help themselves and stay out of the cook's way. If your kitchen is also your calendar control center, is everything you need in one spot, easily accessible, and up to date without expired coupons or old school schedules in the way?

What *should* or *shouldn't* happen here? If you want your kitchen to be a fully functioning work space, then it might be time to move the kids' easel into the playroom. If you eat here, but your table is covered with bills and mail, then that system doesn't work, either. You need another place in the house to toss the day's mail.

As a family, collectively decide on the kitchen's main purposes and write them down on a sheet of paper. Display the paper where you'll see it as you work; this will keep you motivated. You might also want to move your family purpose statement from the living room into the kitchen for the next few days.

Declutter the Counters

Remove all the stuff from your countertops, and put it in one central location (perhaps the same location you used while working in the living room). This includes smaller appliances, bowls of fruit, knife blocks, and wine bottles. Don't forget any meta-stuff you might have. Strip the outside of your fridge naked, too. The only things you should leave are the contents of your refrigerator, your pantry, your cabinets, and your drawers. We'll get to those later. Basically, clear off those things you can see without digging behind closed doors.

Get Rid of Space Hogs and Single Taskers

Kitchens are gadget magnets. It's easy to watch infomercials and gaze in adoration at those magazine ads for gadgets that promise to make your cooking life easier. Eventually, if you're persuaded to buy the thing, you've probably noticed soon after its purchase that the opportunity cost of owning the thing isn't worth the space it consumes.

You really don't need much to run a fully functioning kitchen. Aimée Wimbush-Bourque, a former personal chef and editor of SimpleBites.net, recommends these ten basic items that will equip the average home cook with everything he or she needs:

1. **A good quality knife.** A sharp knife will save you so much time and energy, and it's one of the best investments you can make for your kitchen. Aimée recommends starting with a 6½" (17cm) chef's knife and a small paring knife because about 90 percent of all knife work can be completed with either of these.

2. **Melamine mixing bowls.** A set of three nesting mixing bowls that are durable, lightweight, and heat resistant are useful for most types of cooking and baking. Rubber base rings grip the counter and make these an ideal choice over stainless steel mixing bowls.

3. **Tongs.** Perhaps one of the most useful kitchen tools ever, Aimée says she refers to her tongs as a third hand because she reaches for them so often during the day. Not only are they great for turning meat on the barbecue, they work well to loosen boiling spaghetti (eliminating those unfriendly octopi), toss a salad, turn cubes of browning stew meat or chicken, and to fish out deep-fried nuggets. You can also use them to serve food at the table.

4. **Stainless frying pans.** Heavy enough to sear a steak or dissolve sugar, versatile stovetop-to-oven frying pans are essential for everyday use. Quality ones will last you years before showing any signs of wear and tear.

5. **Large cutting board.** A hefty wooden board has many different uses, ranging from basic, everyday food prep to serving as a cheese board at a party. If you have storage space for it, opt for a large cutting board. You can have three different items in various stages of preparation in three corners of a large board.

6. **Silicone spatula.** Heat resistant to 800° F (427°C), these spatulas are the perfect balance between firm and flexible. The silicone head won't scratch nonstick cookware and is easily removed and tossed in the dishwasher for proper disinfecting.

7. **Fine-mesh sieve.** Perfect for straining sauces, sifting flours, or passing delicate purées, a durable sieve is also great for rinsing rice and beans, washing berries, and straining pulp and seeds out of citrus fruits. A standard 5" (13cm) size will accommodate most cooking uses.

8. **Immersion blender.** A hand blender helps purée soups, whip up batches of salad dressing, emulsify sauces, blend together smoothies, and purée baby food. After a knife, this just may be a kitchen's most versatile tool. Many hand blenders (or stick blenders, as they are also known) also come with several handy attachments, such as a whisk and a chopper that can serve as a mini food processor.

9. **Dutch oven.** From pasta sauces to curries to meaty stews and delicate custards, a quality Dutch oven will last you a lifetime and can be used for nearly any type of cooking. It functions as a slow cooker, a rice pudding pot, a paella pan, and many other one-pot wonders.

10. **Baking sheet.** Useful for more than just cooking, you can use this for drying bread in the oven for bread crumbs, catching vegetable peelings, or holding a mountain of shish kebabs headed for the barbecue. Visit a restaurant store to find the really big cookie sheets; otherwise, don't invest a lot of money on expensive sheets.

There are two other kitchen appliances that can be huge helps if you plan to use them on a regular basis (at least once every week or two).

1. **Coffee grinder.** A small coffee grinder works perfectly for both coffee and for grinding spices. If you buy your spices whole and prefer to grind them yourself, this is a time-saving tool for you. When you switch spices, or go from coffee to cardamom, simply pulse some coarse salt through the grinder to remove odors and then wipe the grinder clean with a dry cloth.

2. **Stand mixer.** If you can afford it, and if you have room for it, this gadget will help you make quality pizza dough, cakes, cookies, and frosting. A hand mixer works just fine, however, so you should only have this if you bake extensively and if you have the room in your kitchen to use it.

Beyond this, do you really need more? You might keep a slow cooker or a coffee pot, but you truly don't need more than this for your

tip If you're truly not sure whether a gadget is useful, write today's date on a sticker and attach the sticker to the bottom of the gadget. If the next time you touch it is more than three months from now, then it's time to say good-bye. It doesn't seem like long, but three months is plenty of time to make good, thorough use of your kitchen space. Many kitchens are small, and it would be a shame to hoard precious storage space for something that is only used annually. Even if your kitchen is large, a rarely used object still isn't worth keeping.

kitchen to work well. If an appliance hasn't seen the light of day in three months, then you probably don't need it. Send it along to charity, post it on Craigslist, or give it to a friend who could use it.

Clean

First, empty your dishwasher and fill it with the dirty dishes, or hand wash your dirty dishes and put them away. Clean any items that need a good washing. The kitchen is bacteria central, so now's the time to really scrub. Use an all-purpose cleaner, and let it sit on the counter for around five minutes to let it wage war on the germs. Soap and water usually kill most germs, and vinegar is even known to have antibacterial properties, so please relax about using chemicals to kill the bacteria. Tea tree essential oil is also antiseptic, and it works wonders on mold (but it is toxic to cats, so use it sparingly if you have felines).

Scrub with a regular scouring pad or sponge (depending on the type of counter surfaces you have), and also use a toothbrush to get edges, corners, and the base of your faucet. Don't forget the outside of the fridge, and give special attention to the door handle. Use a cotton ball and rubbing alcohol if you'd like to really disinfect it.

Remove your stovetop hardware and let it sit in hot, soapy water in your sink. Scrub the stovetop, and if you don't have a self-cleaning oven, clean the inside with homemade oven cleaner (see appendix A) and a scraper. You may need to let the cleaner set overnight.

Wipe down the cabinet doors with a damp cloth and all-purpose cleaner (again, it depends on the surface). If you have real wood cabinets, check with the manufacturer about cleaning procedures.

Use a vacuum or damp cloth to get crumbs out from under the oven, fridge, and between the cabinets. Again, use an old cardboard tube such as a paper towel roll tube if you don't have an attachment.

Clean and disinfect your small appliances with all-purpose cleaner and rubbing alcohol or tea tree oil. For a wood butcher block, rub half a lemon on the surface to disinfect. Let it sit for ten minutes, then rinse.

Organize Your Counters

Put your remaining small appliances back on the countertops, unless you can find room in a cabinet. Storing them out of sight is much more preferable, but house the ones you use daily within easy reach. Think of your countertops as real estate for work space—when you subtract an appliance's home, you're getting more cooking room. Appliances also add visual clutter, so leave them out only if there's no room elsewhere.

The Exterior of the Refrigerator

Display things on the fridge that are truly useful or beautiful. If this is where you keep the family calendar, then update it with important dates, and toss the paper scraps you were using to remind you of these events. Throw away expired coupons, keep only the ones you think you'll use, and transfer them to a simple organizing system of envelopes. Edit your refrigerator magnet collection as well. You don't really need a dozen magnets from your pizza delivery place or the local nail salon.

If all of this was a big job, now's a natural time to call it a day. You can move on to phase two tomorrow.

Declutter the Refrigerator

We're back to decluttering. Empty the refrigerator and freezer of their contents, and toss the science experiments.

Clean

While the good food is sitting out in the open, clean the inside of the fridge with baking soda and warm water. If the drawers are especially questionable, take them out and wash them with soap. Don't forget the rubber seal along the door—that's a favorite place for stuff to collect. Use a cotton ball and rubbing alcohol or tea tree oil to disinfect that area.

Organize

Reshelve the good food, but in logical places. If you need to readjust the shelves in your fridge so that they make more sense, do it now. Make sure all of your leftovers are well labeled—if you're storing them in plastic containers, simply use a dry erase marker directly on the surface to mark the contents and the date it was first stored. Glass is preferable, however, because it lowers the risk of BPA leaching into your food, and

 future project

If you have cheap, business card–style magnets from local stores and cafés, use some glue to cover them with your favorite photos, magazine clippings, and postcards. Create your own little works of art.

tip Kitchens can handle unique wall colors, so brighten up the place with paint for an affordable update. Studies have shown that the colors orange, red, and yellow work well for kitchens because they stimulate the appetite.

it's usually cheaper—save glass jars when you finish your pickles and jelly, and use these for leftover storage.

As you put your bulk food or longer-term items back in the freezer, write out an inventory of what and how much you've got and the general date it was first stored (if you can remember). Then post this somewhere prominently where you can check it when you menu plan. You can find a simple food inventory template in appendix B.

Declutter the Pantry

Remove everything from your pantry—this includes all of your dried goods, even if they're housed in a separate cabinet. Pile them in one central location. Sort through these items, and categorize them in different groups by type—all the cans of vegetables together, the spices and herbs together, and so on. Toss expired items. Remove anything you won't use. You can donate these items to a food bank if they are unopened.

Inventory everything you have left, indicating how much you have either by quantity (i.e., six packets of microwave popcorn) or by a measurable amount (i.e., eight ounces of tomato paste).

Clean

Wipe down your pantry shelves with a damp cloth and all-purpose cleaner. If the shelves need to be lined, add liner.

Organize

Use easy-to-handle meta-stuff for your food storage. I'm a big fan of recycled jars for my pantry—start saving and washing all of your empty jars of jelly, pickles, and olives, and use them for your foodstuffs. Of highest importance are staple ingredients that don't have sealed packages—brown sugar, pecans, chocolate chips, and the like. Make sure you label stuff that isn't obvious! We often tease my mother-in-law for regularly storing baking soda and baking powder in nondescript jars.

Replace your pantry items in logical locations. If you do mostly scratch cooking, put your cooking staples at eye level or within easy reach. Snack items might need to be put up high, especially if you have very young children—but if you have trustworthy, older children, you might want to lower them, so they can get the snacks themselves. Tweak and arrange the pantry until it makes sense for everybody. Chances are,

 future project

Use scrapbook paper to make simple, decorative labels for your storage jars. Simply wrap a strip of paper around the jar, tape it, and label the jar.

you won't have this perfectly figured out by the end of the day, and that's okay. Don't get too sidetracked by this.

Tape your food inventory to the inside of your pantry door, and cross off items as you use them. This way, you won't buy another can of diced tomatoes before using the seventeen you already have.

Declutter the Cabinets and Drawers

Empty all of your cabinets and drawers, and put everything in your central location. Take out all the dishes and servingware, the pots and pans, and the storage containers. If you're not sure you can get this done in one sitting, empty just a few cabinets and drawers at a time. Don't bite off more than you can chew.

If there are any utensils, dishes, or cookware you don't need, put them in the sell or give boxes, and don't forget to price the yard sale items. Save yourself the hassle and price them now.

Match storage lids with their containers. If there are orphaned lids, or if a container doesn't have a lid that fits, get rid of it, or put it to use in your child's play kitchen.

Junk Drawers

Most homes have a designated, this-thing-has-no-obvious-place-so-it-goes-here spot. Mine does. And I'm okay with that. Families need easily accessible rubber bands, stamps, batteries, sticky notes, and extra keys, and a junk drawer is an ideal spot for these things. And because the kitchen is such a central location in a home, it's often the home of this innocuous space.

The most crucial thing about having a junk drawer is clearing it out often. About once a month, empty out the contents and quickly sort through them. Toss the items you don't need, and restock the rest. Do this drawer now, along with your silverware and kitchen towel drawers.

Clean

Wipe down your cabinet shelves and drawers with a damp cloth and all-purpose cleaner. And again, if these shelves need liners, now is the best time to insert them.

Organize

Put your things back in logical places. Cooking utensils should be near the stove. Store pots and pans by the stove as well, where you can easily reach them. Food storage containers are best stored low, where your kids can play. Place mugs and drinking glasses by the refrigerator. Put the forks, spoons, and knives in a drawer where the whole family can easily reach them without disturbing the cook. If you find you now have more room in your cabinets, put some of your seldom-used counter appliances in them. You can still easily bring out your toaster when you need it, but it won't take up space when not in use.

A Final Clean

Sweep and mop your floors with equal parts vinegar and hot water, and add a few drops of essential oil, if you like.

Clean your windows using glass cleaner and newspaper, and clean your blinds in the same way you did in your living room.

Step Back and Evaluate

Is your kitchen enjoyable? Is it fun to cook there? When you have time, take a few steps to revive the place from a cooking utensil catchall to a

 reflection questions

What is the main purpose of your kitchen? How does this area help further your goals represented in your family purpose statement? What can you do to make this space work for each family member? Did you add many kitchen items to your give or sell boxes? If so, what steps might you take so that in the future you won't be tempted to buy kitchen gadgets?

place where meals are created and great conversation is shared. Let your kitchen evolve as you have the time, funds, and as your needs change.

You just did some major work—the kitchen is not an easy place to organize. Celebrate! Open a bottle of wine and enjoy good conversation on the back patio tonight.

Kitchen Checklist:

DECLUTTER
- ☐ Countertops
- ☐ Refrigerator surface
- ☐ Refrigerator and freezer contents
- ☐ Pantry
- ☐ Cabinet contents
- ☐ Drawer contents

CLEAN
- ☐ Counters
- ☐ Stove
- ☐ Oven
- ☐ Cabinet doors
- ☐ Hard-to-reach crevices
- ☐ Small appliances
- ☐ Butcher blocks
- ☐ Refrigerator, inside and out
- ☐ Pantry shelves
- ☐ Cabinet shelves
- ☐ Floor and/or carpet
- ☐ Wash dishes
- ☐ Empty dishwasher
- ☐ Disinfect small appliances
- ☐ Sweep and mop your floors with equal parts vinegar and hot water, and a few drops of essential oil (optional)

ORGANIZE
- ☐ Small appliances
- ☐ Refrigerator
- ☐ Freezer
- ☐ Freezer inventory list
- ☐ Pantry
- ☐ Pantry inventory list
- ☐ Drawers
- ☐ Cabinets

12 | The Bathrooms

"Simplicity is the ultimate
sophistication."

–LEONARDO DA VINCI

Most of today's homes have anywhere from one to three bathrooms, and the homebuilding trend is moving to one bathroom per bedroom—that means one single-family unit could have four bathrooms! In any case, bathrooms are clutter magnets—just think of all those travel-sized

What You'll Need:

CLEANERS

- ☐ All-purpose cleaner*
- ☐ Toilet bowl cleaner*
- ☐ Baking soda
- ☐ Rubbing alcohol
- ☐ Glass cleaner*
- ☐ Vinegar (optional)
- ☐ Mold remover* (optional)
- ☐ Lemon (optional)
- ☐ Essential oil (optional)

TOOLS

- ☐ Trash can
- ☐ Sponge
- ☐ Toothbrush for cleaning
- ☐ Toilet brush
- ☐ Tub brush
- ☐ Cotton balls
- ☐ Newspaper (optional)
- ☐ Microfiber cloth
- ☐ Vacuum
- ☐ Hose attachment for the vacuum
- ☐ Wrapping paper tube or paper towel tube (if you don't have a vacuum attachment)
- ☐ Broom
- ☐ Dustpan
- ☐ Mop
- ☐ Mop bucket
- ☐ Your give and sell boxes
- ☐ Price tags and marker
- ☐ Pen and paper
- ☐ Cotton swabs (optional)
- ☐ Shelf-lining paper (optional)

* Homemade recipes for these cleaners are found in appendix A.

shampoo bottles lurking beneath the sink. Usually, the clutter grows in tandem with the amount of space available, so the more bathrooms you have, the more bathroom "stuff" you own. But not for much longer.

The Game Plan

Today, we're going to clean out everything in your bathrooms, no matter how many you have. Then we're going to reorganize them in a logical way, keeping only the truly necessary things. We'll also be tackling the linen closet, regardless of its location.

What's the Purpose of Your Bathrooms?

What happens in this space? Okay, so there is the painfully obvious. But there are the not-so-obvious tasks that sometime happen in a bathroom as well. There's cleaning and grooming ourselves, but often, a bathroom serves simply as storage space with a mirror on the wall. It's so easy to open the cabinets, toss the little things in, and then close the doors and forget about everything inside. Think about the essential tasks your bathroom serves—bathing, grooming, and using the toilet are it. Should there be any more?

Unless you use something specifically in the bathroom, it really shouldn't belong in this room (unless the linen closet is housed within). Make your bathrooms pleasant, practical places to be in, and eliminate everything else.

Instead of writing down your bathroom's *purpose* (because, really, how specific do we need to get today?), write down a few words that describe the ambience you're after. Do you like a playful mood for your kids' bathroom? For your own bathroom, are you after a spa-like retreat? Your goal today isn't to redecorate, but with a goal like this in mind, you'll be better prepared to toss the things you don't need and keep only the treasures you find beautiful. It'll help you when you're tempted to keep your collection of hotel soaps.

Declutter

Remove everything from your countertops, and put the items in one central location. Also include the stuff from your cabinets, drawers, shelves, shower/tub area, and from under the sink. If you keep medications and cleaners in your bathroom and have young children in your house, temporarily put the toxic items in a separate, safe location far from curious fingers. Basically, what should be left are a tub, a toilet, a sink, a mirror, and a countertop. You might want to do this for all of your bathrooms at one time, bringing all the bathroom knickknacks together—but if your bathrooms are loaded with stuff, tackle them one at a time. It'll backfire if you gather too many items in one place at one time; you'll be overwhelmed and tempted to throw in the towel.

In your central location, sort your bathroom items by category:

Cosmetics and Toiletries
Do you have a lot of half-used bottles? Check their expiration dates—if they're from the Reagan administration, please toss them. If they have just a smidgen of product left, you have a few options. There's no problem with throwing it away. If you're hesitant, perhaps you can

consolidate similar items into one bottle (I had a lot of the same almost-gone shampoos from various hotels, so they easily converged into one travel-sized bottle). Pour the rest of your almost-used liquid soaps into your kids' baths, giving them a few extra bubbles. Get creative—the idea is that you don't need forty-seven small bottles squatting on valuable real estate.

Most people have far more toiletries than they possibly need. A sale on lotion that promises fewer wrinkles or shampoo guaranteed to thicken your hair might sit under your counter for years if you're not careful. Toss everything that's already opened but not being used. It might feel wasteful to toss so many "useful" things, but ask yourself this—why aren't you using it? Are you not crazy about the smell? Have you found something that works better? Whatever the reason, it's probably not going to change, so the only thing the unused product is doing is taking precious space that could be used for things you *do* need and love.

If a product hasn't been opened and is still fresh—yet you have no use for it—add it to your give box. Toiletry items really don't belong at a yard sale, but you could donate them to a battered women's or homeless shelter because they always need these types of items. Check with your local charities, and please donate only unused, sealed items.

Empty your makeup bag, and toss out items that you never use, that are impossible to use (e.g., gummy, so-thick-you-can't-open-it nail polish), or that are a few years old. Get rid of the cosmetics past their expiration date. If you're not sure, but you know it's been a while, it wouldn't hurt to toss it. Organizer Peter Walsh has an easy tip: the closer to the eye the product is applied, the shorter the product's life span. Check the shelf life of your cosmetics with this chart:

Mascara	3–4 months
Foundation, liquid	1 year
Foundation, powder	2 years
Eyeshadow, powder	2 years
Eyeshadow, cream	1 year
Eyeliner, liquid	6 months
Eyeliner, pencil	2 years
Blush, liquid	1 year
Blush, powder	2 years
Lipstick	2 years
Nail polish	2 years

If you have old cosmetics, there must be a reason you're not wearing the product regularly and using it up. Give yourself permission to let it go, and in the future, resolve not to fall for the latest ads that promise thicker lashes or fuller lips. Odds are you have a beauty routine that includes a few staple colors and brands that you faithfully use. Stick to those and skip the rest.

A Word on Toiletry "Necessities"

Skin care and cleaning products are expensive. Sure, an occasional product might work wonders, but most of the time, toiletries are a combination of water, chemicals, and forms of petroleum—that's about it. Ask yourself—are your products really worth the money you spend on them? Do they really live up to their promises?

Our family's answer was "no" to most of the products waiting under our bathroom sink. We went through a toiletry revolution of sorts, and decided that just because we've always used a product in our regular grooming repertoire, that didn't mean we really needed to keep shelling out the dough for it. Slowly, we traded in our conventional products for more nontoxic, frugal, and homemade options. It sounds drastic, but the ingredients we need to make our own toiletries are mostly found in local stores, and they take mere seconds to whip up.

I love that these products can be used by the entire family and that they take up minimal space. In our bathroom, my husband and I share one squeeze bottle of hair cleaner, one bottle of hair clarifier, one bottle of soap, one sponge and we have one razor each. That's all. These products are also chemical free, making them perfectly safe to use on any skin (even a baby's)—and because skin is our largest and most porous organ, it's logical to heed what we slather on it. And finally, these products are incredibly frugal because they mostly use the same common ingredients.

Head to appendix A for recipes for homemade hair care, facial cleanser, toothpaste, and deodorant. Consider slowly switching to these all-natural, homemade toiletries. You'll save money, your home will be healthier, and your bathroom counters will thank you.

Linens

How are your towels? Giving your home a ten-day fresh start is not the time to splurge on a new line of towels, but if yours are thinning or have holes, they could be downgraded to cleaning rags. At the very least, they can be towels for car maintenance, or they can be kept in the garage for outdoor use.

Also reconsider how many towels you actually *need*. Sure, you need extras for guests every now and then, but if you're in the habit of doing laundry weekly, you really only need one towel per family members, plus a few extra. Towels need laundering weekly anyway, and they're sturdy enough to last years. If you have more than you know what to do with, battered women's and homeless shelters often need good towels. So if you decide to minimize your towel supply, put them in your give box.

If you store sheets in your linen closet, sort through them. If any are old, dingy, or no longer fit any beds in your home, they can be repurposed as floor coverings for painting projects and kids' activities. You can also cut them into squares to be used as cleaning rags. But if you have no use for the extra sheets, don't keep them around—toss them in your give box.

Take inventory of how many sheets you have in each size and write it down. Hold on to this inventory list, because you'll use it as you reorganize your linen closet soon. You can find a simple inventory template in appendix B.

Clean

Use all-purpose cleaner and a cleaning cloth to wipe down the shelves in your linen closet, and if necessary, line them with shelf paper. Do the same thing with your shelves under your bathroom cabinet. Use mold remover if the corners look dingy.

Spray all-purpose cleaner on the bathroom counter, and let it sit for a few minutes to kill the germs. Use a regular scouring pad or sponge (depending on the type of your countertop surface), and use a toothbrush to get edges, corners, and the base of your faucet. A simple cotton swab will remove grime from difficult crevices in the faucet. If you want to scrub your counters, sprinkle them with baking soda, which will give you a scouring effect without chemicals.

If you have any countertop stains, cut a lemon in half and scrub the stain with the open side of the lemon. Let it rest until the lemon juice dries, and then rinse it off—the stain should disappear.

Clean and disinfect the items that belong on your bathroom counter, such as your soap dispenser and toothbrush holder.

Use toilet bowl cleaner and a toilet brush to clean the toilet, making sure to get around all the sides.

Wipe down the cabinet doors with a damp cloth and all-purpose cleaner. Again, if you have real wood cabinets, consult the manufacturer's instructions for proper cleaning.

Clean your bathtub and tile with basic baking soda and a sponge or tub brush. If it needs a really good cleaning, first soak the difficult areas in vinegar—but use it sparingly because vinegar can break down grout. For mold issues, use homemade mold remover (see appendix A). Spray the affected area, wait at least an hour, and then rinse it off.

If there are bath toys for your children, clean and disinfect them with rubbing alcohol or tea tree oil.

Clean the mirrors with glass cleaner and a microfiber cloth or crumpled newspaper.

Use a vacuum or damp cloth to get grime and dust out from behind the toilet, between the cabinets, and around the vanity and other hard-to-reach places.

Sweep and mop your floors with equal parts vinegar and hot water, and add a few drops of essential oil.

Organize

Use labeled containers to house your small-sized products under the bathroom counter—and if you use containers with lids, they'll be stackable. Separate your toiletries and supplies by type, and store them in small, portable containers. If you choose to go the homemade route, store the ingredients under the counter—they'll be easy to access when you need to quickly whip up a fresh batch.

Label your containers well, and protect them from moisture. Covering simple paper labels with clear packing tape does the trick.

Keep *only* the bathing toiletries you use daily in your bathtub or shower. If there's room under the counter for a basket of bath toys, keep them there. Otherwise, find a waterproof container to store bath toys on the side of the bathtub.

If you don't have them yet, attach simple-yet-sturdy hooks to the wall to be used for drying towels. Go for the metal variety found at home improvement stores instead of the plastic, peel-and-stick types, which won't last long. Hang the hooks near the shower, and assign one to each person. Label the hooks if it will help family members remember where their towels go. Make it a habit in your family to hang each

tip   Dollar stores are a great place to find plastic storage containers. Shoeboxes also work well. If you're into aesthetics, you can always wrap them in wallpaper remnants; it's more water-resistant than scrapbook paper or gift wrap.

person's towel on his or her assigned hook after a shower or bath. This way, you won't use more towels than you need, which will help your laundry loads go down in size.

Refold your linens, and shelve them in a logical way. If you grab sheets or towels on a regular basis, put them within easy reach. Keep only what you need within reach. If you keep twenty towels at arm's length, your family will use more than they need. Store one per person in an easy-to-reach location, and store any extras a shelf or two higher.

How To Fold a Fitted Sheet

1. Spread out your fitted sheet face down.

2. Fold it in half widthwise, and tuck the bottom two corners into the top two corners.

3. Next, fold the sheet across, tucking all four corners into each other.

4. Straighten the sheet, and then fold a side one-third into the center.

Store matching sheets and pillowcases together—keep them in a well-labeled or transparent bag, or even in one of the pillowcases, so the set is easy to find. You can also tie the set together with simple twine, adding a tag that labels the sheet size.

Use the photos to help you fold fitted sheets, the arch nemesis of an organized linen closet.

Tape your linen inventory on the inside of the closet door so that you have an idea of what's available and whether you need to buy more.

5. Fold the other third into the center.

6. Next, fold the bottom third up to the middle.

7. Finally, fold the top third over.

8. A fitted sheet, perfectly folded.

reflection question

Refer back to the descriptive words you wrote down at the beginning of today's tasks. Does your bathroom live up to these words? Don't spend an outrageous amount on a teak dressing bench or a silver-plated soap dispenser, but small touches—such as a naturally scented candle, good-smelling hand soap, and lotion on the counter—make a bathroom inviting and cozy. A basket of rolled-up towels creates a nice hotel look. Lighting affects a room's mood, so a dimmer switch is an inexpensive way to add some coziness and romance. If your bathroom is frustratingly dark, put a small desk lamp on the corner of the counter.

Ultimately, a simple bathroom is the way to go. If it has only the bare essentials, it will look clean, uncluttered, and relaxing. If you're not sure whether a decorative item adds to the look, remove it for a week or two. If you get used to the bathroom without it, you have your answer. But if you include it and like the addition, then keep it and enjoy it.

Bathroom Checklist:

DECLUTTER

- ☐ Countertop items
- ☐ Items under the counter
- ☐ Items in other cabinets
- ☐ Linen closet
- ☐ Items in the bathtub
- ☐ Items in the medicine cabinet
- ☐ Items on shelves
- ☐ _____
- ☐ _____
- ☐ _____
- ☐ _____

CLEAN

- ☐ Shelves in the linen closet
- ☐ Linen closet floor
- ☐ Bathroom counter
- ☐ Items on your bathroom counter
- ☐ Cabinet doors
- ☐ Shelves under the bathroom counter
- ☐ Toilet
- ☐ Bathtub
- ☐ Mirrors
- ☐ Bathroom floor
- ☐ _____
- ☐ _____
- ☐ _____
- ☐ _____
- ☐ _____
- ☐ _____
- ☐ _____
- ☐ _____

ORGANIZE

- ☐ Linens in the linen closet
- ☐ Towels
- ☐ Toiletries
- ☐ Bath toys
- ☐ Medicine cabinet
- ☐ Makeup
- ☐ _____
- ☐ _____
- ☐ _____
- ☐ _____
- ☐ _____

13 | The Kids' Rooms

"If your mind isn't clouded by unnecessary things, this is the best season of your life."

–WU-MEN

Children value different things than adults do. They'll line the window-sills of their rooms with rocks, wallpaper the backs of their doors with scribbles, and collect wildflowers in drinking glasses. They often value toys we don't quite understand—the seven My Little Ponies that all look the same, except for their color; the Transformers they beg for every time you're in the store.

Given the right environment, you can give your children a safe haven for their treasures without helping them needlessly hoard or value things more than relationships. As their parent, you can make your kids' rooms spaces that reflect your family's values—where they can grow, seek solitude, enjoy their belongings, and find contentment with what they already have.

What you'll need:

CLEANERS

- ☐ All-purpose cleaner*
- ☐ Glass cleaner*
- ☐ Rubbing alcohol
- ☐ Baking soda (optional)
- ☐ Vinegar (optional)
- ☐ Essential oil (optional)

TOOLS

- ☐ Trash can
- ☐ Boxes for clothes storage
- ☐ Sponge
- ☐ Cotton balls
- ☐ Microfiber cloth
- ☐ Vacuum (or broom, dustpan, and mop depending on your floor type)
- ☐ Paper and pen
- ☐ Your give and sell boxes
- ☐ Price tags and marker

* Homemade recipes for these cleaners are found in appendix A.

The Game Plan

Round up the kids because it's good for them to help you with this task. Treat them with some of their favorite music while you work, and keep their jobs as lighthearted and enjoyable as possible.

What's the Purpose of Your Kids' Rooms?

Sure, your children's rooms serve to store their stuff and give them a place to sleep at night. But is your setup logical? Does it work? Ask yourself—and your family—a few questions that will help trigger ideas for the best system for your kids' living situations.

1. Do your kids need to share or split up rooms?

If your kids each have their own rooms, yet fight continually over toys, perhaps your family might work better with one bedroom and one playroom for your kids. Or do your kids share a room, but are reaching an age where they could use some privacy or where their interests are starting to part ways? Maybe it's time to give them their own rooms, each with their individual toys and books.

2. Are family-shared toys and supplies accessible to everyone?

Most families have one set of art supplies and a shared collection of books. Perhaps you also share most of the toys—the blocks, the dolls, and the dress-up clothes are available to all the children. Are these things accessible to everyone? If one child has toys in his or her room, with the other siblings denied some freedom with these shared items, it's probably best to have a more family-friendly space for these toys. Do your best to keep art supplies, books, and toys for everyone in one neutral space. It will lessen the sibling quarrels, and it will provide a more cooperative playing environment.

3. Do your kids have a good relationship with each other?

Do your children play well together? Do they share friends during playdates? Is there a sense of friendship between the siblings? Your living space might be helping—or hindering—their relationship. If you value relationships over things, think through some issues your children have with each other. Does a particular child need a corner of his or her own? Could your daughters gain more appreciation for each other by sharing clothes and living space? Evaluate your family's harmony, and make plans to strengthen it through your living environment.

As you answer these questions, you'll be better able to define the purpose of all the rooms your kids use. Decide together what each room's purpose is, and write it down to display as you work. Remind the kids of your family purpose statement as well.

Declutter the Clothing Stash

Go through each of your children's clothes, and set aside items that no longer fit. If there are siblings down the line who can wear the old clothes (or if you think there might be in the future), store the clothes organized by size and gender. If you won't need them in the next year, store them somewhere like the garage or the attic (but be aware that in a hot climate, fabric can yellow). Label the boxes well. Cardboard boxes can work, but large plastic containers with snap-shut lids protect clothes from potential bug infestations and weather changes. They're worth the investment.

You're left with the clothes that fit your children *now*, or will fit them within the year. Sort these remaining clothes by season, and store the off-season clothes in boxes. Again, cardboard will work, but plastic containers will hold up to wear and tear and should last years. Don't store these seasonal clothes too far away because you'll use them in a few months. A good spot is the shelves at the top of your child's closet, if you're blessed to have this space.

Go through your kids' socks and match pairs. Orphaned socks can either be tossed or made into sock puppets or dust rags.

As you're sorting through clothes, write down a basic inventory, and take note of what you'll need this next year. You can find a basic clothing inventory in appendix B.

What Do They Really Need?

Children, especially very young children, go through clothes before they can possibly wear out or go out of style. This is the beauty of saving older siblings' clothing for younger children down the road because the clothing staples can be a one-time purchase. But this same philosophy can be applied while you're shopping for *more* clothes. Because children grow so fast, secondhand stores are optimum places to find great pieces at reasonable prices. Here are a few tips for finding what your family needs each year, all at discounted prices.

1. Go in with a plan … Before shopping, know ahead of time what you need. Sometimes thrift stores can be a bit overwhelming, and each location has its own organizing system, making it challenging to find what you need. So if you know you're looking for 12–24-month-old boy's khakis, and size 8 black dress shoes, it can be a lot less stressful. Take the inventory sheet you created as you went through your current stash of kids' clothing.

2. ... But be open-minded. Go with a plan, but keep your eyes open for any surprising deals. Because the stock is constantly changing, it's hit or miss with thrift stores, and sometimes you really hit the jackpot. If you weren't necessarily shopping for swimsuits, but you see a darling one in your daughter's size for next summer, then snag it. You need to make sure what you find is something you *actually* need; otherwise, you're just buying clutter, and you're not saving money.

3. Look for quality brands ... I'm not a fan of cheaply made clothing. You may think you're getting a deal, but if the item is going to shrink or fade after one washing, or if the buttons pop off after a bit of rough play, then that piece of clothing isn't going to last more than one kid, and perhaps no more than a few months. But the beauty of thrift store shopping is that if the majority of your wardrobe comes from these stores, you can afford great quality brands. You'd be surprised by the amount of well-made, expensive clothing hiding in thrift shops, just waiting to be found. You have to dig for it, but it's there. My kids can wear babyGap and Gymboree, thanks to thrift stores.

4. ... But also try new brands. Keep in mind, however, that there might be some quality pieces in brands you've never heard of or with the tags completely missing. Check for holes, stains, missing buttons, and loose seams, and pass on something if it looks pretty worn or stretched out. Sometimes the brands you don't know are actually high-end European brands, well worth the money.

5. Don't go with the kids. Sure, you may have to bring them sometimes. But if you're armed with a detailed list, it can be hard to get much accomplished at a thrift store when you have little ones to watch. If you have to bring your kids, plan on shopping in only one of the store's sections so your time in the store is as short as possible. Then come back another day to shop the rest.

6. Know your local store's sale days. Many stores have half-off days once a week. Call your local store and ask for its regular sale schedule. Some have copies of their sales schedules available at their registers.

7. Stockpile; think long-term. We actually don't need to buy clothes for our kids for a long time because my mother-in-law has containers of boys and girls clothes of all sizes waiting to be grown into. She stops by thrift stores weekly and is always on the lookout for clothes for her grandkids. We're probably set for at least two years because she thinks long-term when she thrift shops. If you have the storage to stockpile, then consider your family's long-term needs. Don't overbuy, however; keep your list of needs with you at all times.

8. Go often. If you don't find anything one week, try again a few weeks later. A thrift store's inventory changes constantly, so you might strike gold one week and come up with nothing the next. Make thrift store shopping part of your regular home management routine.

9. Go with cash. Finally, leave your debit card at home. When you're armed with cash, you'll be more selective with your purchases and will therefore think more levelheadedly about the value of items. When you stick to a budget, thrift stores are a money-saver. When you go way over, you're buying more than you need, which not only empties your wallet but also overfills your closets.

Clean the Closets

While the closet and dresser are somewhat empty, dust them with a microfiber cloth. Sweep or vacuum the closet floor, and check the corners and the back of the dresser for cobwebs.

Organize the Closets

Reshelve and rehang your kids' clothes in a way that gives your kids as much independence as possible. Are clothes hanging on a dowel rod that is too high for them to reach? Lower them to your child's arm reach; this way, she can learn the important task of getting herself ready for the day. Make it easy for your kids to put their clothes away, too. If your kids are small, keep a step stool in the closet to help them reach and return things properly. Your child's closet is a good place to let go of perfectionism and to let her store clothes in a way that works for both you and her, as long as it keeps the room tidy. It will teach her independence and self reliance. Cotton or other natural weave clothing will stand up to a bit of crumpling and jamming into drawers.

Declutter the Toys

Prepare for some possible emotional battles as you tackle the toys. Go through *all* toys, and question each one. Do your kids still play with them? Do they have missing pieces? Are they broken? Basically, which toys are beautiful or useful to them?

If a toy is completely unusable for whatever reason, get rid of it. If one child no longer plays with it, perhaps a younger sibling might want it in the near future. If so, keep it, but store it out of sight until it's age-appropriate for the younger one. With little children, ask the simple question, "Do you still want to play with this?" They might say yes, even though you know it's never played with. Set it aside for now, and when you've finished questioning all of their toys, ask them to reevaluate these toys. If they still say yes, designate a container to store these toys out of sight for a few weeks. Then rotate these with the toys you've left out. With little kids, seeing a toy after a brief bit of absence is like receiving a brand-new toy. Or you might discover that your kids don't miss the toys they were sure they loved. If they never ask about a toy, then store it away for a younger sibling, or put it in your give or sell box. E-Bay and Craigslist are godsends for selling toys, so if you think an unloved toy has some value, put it on the market. Because you've got a yard sale on the horizon, price all of these toys for sale—they sell well at yard sales.

A final option is to donate unused toys to charity. This is a good opportunity to teach your kids about giving to those less fortunate and to nurture a compassionate heart. As you sort through the toys, talk about this idea, and involve them in the process. But don't force them to donate their toys with the "there-are-starving-children-in-Africa-who-would-love-to-have-this" line.

What Do They Really Need?

Children need far fewer toys than mainstream media would have us believe. Maria Montessori was an Italian educator at the end of the nineteenth century and the beginning of the twentieth century, and also happened to be the first female doctor in Italy. Her driving interest was in the psychology behind special-needs and extremely poor children, who in those days were not given much of an education. When she studied these kids' behavior, she found that even without toys, children would invent creative games and make-believe with the crumbs on the floor. Denied toys, these children *still* found ways to play.

Most of our children are blessed enough not to need to play with crumbs, but we've all witnessed this theory. Kids will play outside for hours with sticks and rocks. A toddler is more fascinated with the box the toy came in than the actual toy. Even after receiving new toys for birthdays or Christmas, children often resort to playing with their tried-and-true favorites after a few weeks.

This is more than merely interesting—it should serve as a sobering reminder that our children could actually benefit from fewer toys, not more. The fewer toys a child has, the more inventive she has to be. And when she's inventive, she's using her imagination and her creativity, which stimulates her brain.

The same is true with the *type* of toys children play with. When a toy does more, the child does less. If a toy talks to the child, moves and sings, and creates the story line for playtime, the child doesn't have to do much more than watch and be entertained. The toy is doing more playing than the child. Open-ended toys allow for longer creative play, spanning both genders, with a large age range. Opt for these kind of quality, long-lasting, open-ended toys. My favorites are:

1. **Wooden blocks.** A simple set of blocks in different shapes and sizes opens the door to hours of creative play for years.
2. **Dolls.** Kids only need a few dolls, but if they're quality and well made, they'll last generations.

3. **Art supplies.** Crayons, markers, colored pencils, construction paper, scrap printer paper, glue sticks, safety scissors, stickers ... kids can invent thousands of uses for each of these things.

4. **Dress-up clothes.** Last year's Halloween costumes, hand-me-downs that no one wears, and old-fashioned clothing found in Grandma's attic can all be saved for a dress-up trunk.

5. **Play kitchens and food.** You can easily reuse empty food containers and secondhand kitchen supplies, but I think it's also worth the money to invest in decent play food. Wooden and cloth play food lasts the longest. You can find some great felted or knitted play food on Etsy.com.

6. **Building toys.** Tinkertoys and other types like this provide hours of open-ended entertainment and stretch kids' reasoning skills.

7. **Board games.** Games are great for interaction, for learning about following directions and taking turns, and for learning how to win and lose graciously.

8. **Cars and trucks.** Boys love to race and maneuver these vehicles during their playtime, but girls enjoy these as well. Simple Matchbox cars will last a long time, usually spanning generations.

Clean

Dust and wipe down your toy storage system with an all-purpose cleaner; this includes the toy box, the shelves, and the baskets. Clean the toys, too; disinfect them with a cotton ball and some rubbing alcohol.

Dust the rest of the room with a microfiber cloth, and clean surfaces with all-purpose cleaner. If there are crayon markings anywhere, gently rub the area with baking soda and a sponge. If there are stubborn stickers on the doors or walls, dampen them with vinegar, wait fifteen minutes, and remove them with a sponge.

Have your children help clean. This is one of the great benefits of using nontoxic cleaners. Even small kids can follow behind you and "help" with a spray bottle of water and a clean rag or sponge.

Organize the Toys

Do you have a good storage system for toys? You don't have to spend much money, but it helps to store toys so that kids can find them for playtime and then put them away on their own.

I love the system our family has crafted out of shelves and buckets from IKEA. I labeled the buckets with photos of the toys that belong in each bucket—helpful for children who don't yet read. It's not 100 percent

 future project

If your kids love drawing, painting, or crafting, set aside a special corner, cabinet, or container for art. Make it accessible (within reason, of course), and christen an area in the home an art gallery. A simple bulletin board, a wire on the wall with clothespins, or even the refrigerator works well. For more inspiration, I highly recommend *The Creative Family* by Amanda Soule.

foolproof, but this storage solution has really helped our sanity. If you don't want to spend money, you can also use simple cardboard boxes.

For toys with small pieces, simple mesh or zippered bags can hold them all together. It also helps if these bags are see-through. These are great for puzzle pieces, small doll paraphernalia, or action figure pieces. You can reuse the plastic sleeves that come with the sets of socks and underwear you buy for your kids.

You can also use simple resealable bags for storing small-pieced toys, but plan to replace them every few months because of holes and tears.

Declutter the Books

I am a book fanatic, and I am so thankful my mother saved almost all of my books from childhood. But let's face it—some children's books are just twaddle. *Twaddle* is a term coined by Charlotte Mason, a governess and teacher in late nineteenth and early twentieth centuries England. It means, "dumbed-down literature, absent of meaning."[16] Keep this definition in mind when you sort through your children's books.

 future project

If you don't want bare cardboard boxes for storing toys, have your children decoupage them with wrapping paper, wallpaper, or scrapbook paper. They can also add their own embellishments.

Twaddle might be free gifts in a prepackaged kids' meal, books inconsistent with your family's values, or ridiculous cartoon episodes transcribed in written form. Just as you wouldn't let your children sit in front of the TV and watch just anything, don't stock their shelves with just any book. Only bring home quality. I'd rather have five brilliantly written and illustrated children's books that have stood the test of time than fifty books of plain silliness. Our children deserve quality literature.

Sell, donate, or toss any books that your children don't love, that are poorly written, or that promote a message with which you don't agree. It's painful at first, but once you get going, it's pretty satisfying. I love looking at our children's books and knowing I'm perfectly fine with my kids reading any and all of them.

If you end up with a large stack of books to sell, check their going price at Amazon.com or Half.com. Sometimes books sell quite well on these sites, so you may want to set up a seller's account and list them. But if they're selling for mere pennies, check with a local used bookstore to see what price they offer you. If it's still not a great deal, price your books low for your yard sale. Books don't sell for high prices at yard sales. If your books don't sell at your yard sale, then return to the used bookstore and accept their low offer, or simply donate the books to a local charity.

Don't be so quick with the books that are falling apart or the ones that aren't appropriate for your children's age. Books are repairable, and even the most well-loved books are still readable. My daughter religiously reads a book that was printed in 1963 and was already loved several times over before I faithfully read the book in the '70s. It is really falling apart—its pages are taped together—but it's still a family favorite.

Clean the Bookshelves

Dust and clean the bookshelves with all-purpose cleaner, taking care to get the corners.

Organize the Books

Reshelve the books, making them easy for your children to reach. Children tend to reshelve books wherever they want, so consider how important it is for you to have your books in a particular place. We have a *lot* of children's books, so it's actually important to me that they're in a proper place. In doing so, we can find the exact book we're after. For now, the system that works for us is a simple basket next to the bookshelves, where read books are discarded. This mimics the system most public libraries use. At the end of the day, I reshelve the books as part of my cleaning process. It's worth it to me.

If this isn't important to you, a simple shelf loaded with books is fine. Do what works for your kids.

Clean

Give your kids' rooms a final cleaning by sweeping and mopping, or by vacuuming. Clean any windows and blinds using the same procedure outlined in chapter 10.

reflection questions

Are your children's rooms stimulating? Are they a haven for learning, growing, and for kids to be themselves in? The rooms don't need to be catalog worthy, but a little paint works wonders. Ask your kids what their "dream" bedroom looks like, and consider doing one reasonable thing from their wish list in the next few months.

Kids' Rooms Checklist:

DECLUTTER
- ☐ Clothing
- ☐ Closet
- ☐ Toys
- ☐ Toy storage
- ☐ Books
- ☐ Bookshelves
- ☐ The rest of the bedroom

- ☐ Bookshelves
- ☐ Ceiling fan
- ☐ Crown molding
- ☐ Baseboards
- ☐ Doors
- ☐ Doorknobs
- ☐ Other furniture
- ☐ The rest of the bedroom

CLEAN
- ☐ Closet
- ☐ Dresser
- ☐ Toys
- ☐ Toy storage
- ☐ Books (repair, if necessary)

ORGANIZE
- ☐ Clothes
- ☐ Toys
- ☐ Books
- ☐ Art supplies

DAY 9:

14 | The Master Bedroom

"The secret of happiness, you see, is not found in seeking more, but in developing the capacity to enjoy less."

—DON MILLMAN

We've all heard it before—your bedroom is supposed to be your sanctuary. It needs to be the place you retreat to when you need respite from the world, and it should be calming, inviting, and restful. I'd love to have a room like this, too. But when you're in the trenches of parenthood, it's not surprising in the least to find toy cars under the bed, mountains of laundry waiting for you to scale, or a trail of cracker crumbs from that personalized early morning breakfast call.

Today, we're going to steer through the clutter, make decisions about what's really necessary, and take a few steps toward making your bedroom a bit more of a haven—with or without kids.

The Game Plan

For many of us, the master bedroom is the catchall for clutter when company arrives, and it's often the last room that gets cleaned. Today, we'll give this room the attention it deserves. Both you and your spouse should be as involved as possible in revamping this room. Perhaps set

What You'll Need:

CLEANERS

☐ All-purpose cleaner*

TOOLS

☐ Microfiber cloth

☐ Vacuum or broom, dustpan, and mop

☐ Your give and sell boxes

☐ Price tags and marker

☐ Cleaning cloth

* A homemade recipe for this cleaner is found in appendix A.

aside an evening or an afternoon for your kids with a babysitter so that you can work without interruption.

What's the Purpose of Your Bedroom?

Your bedroom is a very important space. It's the first thing you see in the morning and the last thing you see at night, so it is vital for you to decide what this space is *about*. What is the purpose of your master bedroom? Is it a retreat for you and your spouse? Does it serve a double purpose—office, workout station, library? Some professional organizers and decorators advocate keeping the master bedroom solely dedicated as a bedroom, and of all the rooms in the house, *this* one should be guarded as a peaceful retreat. I agree, in an ideal world. But in reality, some homes are short on space, and almost every room needs to have a double purpose. If you can, keep this room only as your bedroom. But if you can't, make a deliberate decision about what else has to happen here. Try to avoid housing stressful activities, such as bill paying, here.

I recommend not making the room's secondary purpose a laundry room. It's stressful, not restful, to look at piles of clothes that need washing or folding. If this is the best place for you to run on your treadmill, then make sure you have the space to store your equipment effectively; don't make the treadmill a permanent sculpture in your décor or a rack for excess clothing. Only keep exercise equipment here if you've got the room for it. The same is true if your bedroom's secondary purpose is a home office. Keep your desk as small as possible, and opt for one that closes when it's not in use so that you don't have work and bills staring at you while you drift off to sleep.

Once you decide the main purposes of your master bedroom, you'll be able to decide what items must stay, what has to go, and what boundaries to establish so that this room remains some form of oasis for your soul. Write down the room's purpose, and display it somewhere today to keep you motivated as you work.

Declutter the Closets

You've heard this advice before, but it's true— if you haven't worn an item in a year, you really don't need to keep it. Go through your closet, and without overanalyzing, pull out the clothes that fit this category. Leave the clothes you wear on a regular basis, along with a few key pieces you wear only occasionally. Have your spouse do the same with his or her clothes.

Sort through the pile of clothes you haven't worn in a year. There's a good reason you choose not to wear them— they don't fit you well, something about the color just isn't right, the stains or tears make the clothes inappropriate virtually anywhere. Perhaps you bought an item in 1992, and you just can't let it go.

You have permission to get rid of these things. When you donate or sell the items that are in decent shape, you're giving them a second life. I guarantee you won't miss them once they're gone. By getting rid of them, think of what you're choosing to have instead—more closet space for the items you love.

Do the same thing with your jewelry, your bags, and your shoes. It might hurt at first, but I promise, it's like removing a Band-Aid. Declutter quickly, and it'll be over before you know it.

What Do I Really Need?

It's hard to know what to keep and what should go, especially if items are in decent condition. Analyze your stage of life, because this plays a large role in determining your wardrobe. Do you work outside the home, visiting clients, and need to look professional? Are you a stay-at-home parent and spend most time out of the house at the park or at the grocery store? Do you work full-time from home?

Let your wardrobe reflect your stage of life *right now*. Resist the temptation to keep the power suits you *might* use again once the kids are in school. You don't know for sure if you will use them, and chances are, they will be outdated by the time they see the light of day again. Here are a few tips for choosing the absolute best pieces for your wardrobe.

1. Stick with the classics. You'll get much more mileage out of a few versatile, timeless pieces than a closet full of trendy wear. Fashion expert Tim Gunn, author of *A Guide to Quality, Taste, and Style*, recommends these ten items as the essentials for any woman's wardrobe:[17]

1. Basic black dress
2. Trench coat
3. Classic dress pants
4. Classic white shirt
5. Jeans
6. Cashmere sweater
7. Skirt
8. Day dress
9. Blazer
10. Sweat suit alternative

This is a good list, for the most part. I'm definitely not a fashion guru, but in my opinion, a cashmere sweater might be a bit unrealistic for women with small children. Because our clothing gets smeared and splattered as much as our children's, this piece might best wait a few years until your kids are past the messy stage. A well-fitting sweater in cotton, however, is an ideal alternative.

I would also add quality T-shirts to the list, both long-sleeved and short. Well-fitting T-shirts are a mom's uniform, and they work with classic jeans, skirts, and under jackets and blazers. If you have babies and small children, keep a few inexpensive shirts that you wear *only* in the house, because they *will* get stained. They should still fit you well, however. Then invest in beautifully tailored T-shirts in a variety of flattering colors, and take good care of them so that they last.

In addition, I would add a classic cardigan (so that you can get more mileage out of warm-weather shirts), comfortable-but-stylish flats (beyond your flip-flops), and quality, supportive undergarments. Well-fitting undergarments are worth the investment because they'll last years, keep you comfortable all day, and shave pounds off your appearance. Most stores specializing in underwear offer a bra-fitting service. Take advantage of this.

What about men? There isn't as universal a list for men, probably because men have a broader range of environments in which they work, play, and relax. Many men need to wear suits every day to work, but just as many can wear jeans and flip-flops on the job. And if they do need to dress formally during the day, they still need casual wear for evenings and weekends. As the trend veers toward casual living, it's hard to know what clothing exactly *is* necessary.

I took my own informal poll of a group of men, representing a wide range of ages and occupations, and asked them their opinions on the top ten items necessary in a man's wardrobe. The most common results were:

1. A suit in any neutral color except black, paired with a solid-colored tie
2. A long-sleeved button-down shirt in white
3. A long-sleeved button-down shirt in a solid color or a tasteful print
4. Jeans (the darker the rinse, the more versatile the wear)
5. Short-sleeved T-shirts
6. Dress shoes, black and brown
7. Belts, black and brown
8. V-necked sweater in a solid color
9. Khaki pants
10. Short-sleeved polo shirt in a solid color

Following in at a close eleven and twelve were athletic shoes and a classic wool coat. And both should be included in the essential list, in my opinion. Add to the wardrobe a handful of short-sleeved, crew neck white undershirts, underwear, and both athletic and dress socks, and that covers the essentials.

2. Opt for quality over quantity. I would rather have two pairs of jeans that fit me amazingly than ten pairs that fit me so-so. Think about what you grab when you're headed out to run errands. It's typically one of the same pairs of jeans and one of five or so shirts, right? What about a date night? I'll bet money that you almost always go for your favorite pair of jeans, your most flattering skirt, or your most versatile dress. In other words, a large portion of our clothing goes unworn.

Given a choice, we'll *always* wear the articles of clothing that fit us best, make us feel the most comfortable, and are the most flattering to our figures. Why take up useful closet space holding onto those jeans from college that you hope one day may fit again? Why keep that sweater you've never worn because it's a garish color on you, but it was on sale and you couldn't pass it up? There's no logical reason to hold onto items that we honestly know we won't wear. Release the emotional attachment to clothing and accessories, and treat them as what they are—things.

If you're not crazy about most of your clothing, then keep the stuff you wear most often and get rid of the rest. Then make a plan to slowly replace what you did keep, one item for another. When you finally find jeans that fit you perfectly, bring them to your closet and then remove your old pair.

Yes, opting for quality over quantity typically means you'll pay a bit more money for dress pants or a jacket, but not all the time. As I mentioned in chapter 13, thrift stores are a great place to score name-brand pieces at decent prices. Head to the thrift stores in the nicest neighborhood in your city because those tend to have the best items.

But even if you do pay more money, it often means you'll save money in the long run. If higher quality means more expensive, it probably also means it's longer lasting and better fitting. A well-fitting shirt could last you years, while a cheap one might need replacing after a year.

3. Know your colors and your body shape. If you simply don't know what looks good on you, find out. Ask a friend who always dresses well if she could help you sort through your closet. If you always get compliments about a certain sweater, evaluate why. Is it the color? The cut? The pattern? Take notes.

Color Me Beautiful by Carole Jackson is a classic book that explains the four different seasons of color that all people fall into. It has a simple test that will tell you your season. Find the book at your local bookstore or library and use your test results as a basic springboard for learning more about your best colors. The book is thirty years old, but its information is timeless.

Clean the Closets

Attack those dust bunnies in your closet with fury, and clean those shelves and baseboards from highest to lowest with all-purpose cleaner. Finish off with the vacuum.

Organize the Closets

Before you go and buy the latest expensive closet organizing system, first find any unused shelves or boxes in your home. If you *do* need to buy shelves, think outside the box and look in a variety of stores. Hardware stores might have what you need much more cheaply than stores specializing in home goods.

Work *with* your space. If you have more horizontal closet space, hang most of your clothes, including T-shirts. If your closet is minuscule, fold and store your basic items in a dresser. Make your clothes easy to find, which will reduce any haphazard storage tendencies. If you hang your clothes by color, then it won't be too difficult to grab that particular red shirt you're after. It might sound like a hassle, but it only takes a few minutes of initial organizing and then developing the habit of hanging clothes back in the correct spot. In addition to hanging by color, I also like to hang all like items together—all the shirts together, then the pants, then the skirts, and then the jackets. Some people prefer to organize by style or purpose, such as hanging work clothes and weekend wear separately, or even by season, keeping sleeveless shirts and sweaters in their respective areas. Do what works for you.

Shoe storage is a challenge, but there are lots of decent options. You can keep the boxes your shoes came in and store the shoes inside. Over-the-door shoe holders are useful because they take advantage of oft-unused space. If you have shelf space in your closet, you can simply store shoes there. You can also find shoe racks that sit on your closet floor and shoe organizers that hang from a rod. Keep your shoes easy to find so you don't have to hunt for matching pairs when you're running late.

 ## future project

I understand not wanting to part with the plethora of T-shirts from your college days. Cut out the main parts of the shirts you like, and sew them into a casual throw blanket. Stitch them together, either neatly or randomly, and attach a soft fabric, such as flannel, as a simple backing. Now you can curl up and read a book in all of your favorite T-shirts at once.

Make sure you have a logical spot for your dirty clothes. This might be in your laundry room, or you could keep a basket or a hamper in your closet. Make your system easily accessible so that it gets used and doesn't encourage a huge buildup of laundry.

Finally, here's the most important rule in closet organization: Don't try to defy the laws of physics. You simply can't house three-feet worth of T-shirts on an eighteen-inch closet rod. Work with the space you have, and use that as your measuring stick for how vast your wardrobe should be. If you're blessed with abundant closet space, resist the temptation to cram it full of clothes just because you can. Enjoy that excess space for something else, such as craft or hobby storage.

Set a maximum limit on clothing and accessories. Stay under this limit by following this rule: When you add to your collection, get rid of something else, by either selling it or donating it to charity. Stick to your magic number, and you'll never run out of closet space.

Declutter the Room

How's everything else in your bedroom? Are your nightstands overflowing with clutter? Pare down to just those few items you really need before and after sleep—a clock, a lamp, a book, a journal, a pen, and perhaps a treat like a candle or a framed photo. Create some ambience near your bed. It's where you sleep most nights of the year; make it a place you enjoy.

Do you store things under the bed? Pull them all out, and give each item a dusting with a microfiber cloth. Under the bed is a good storage spot, but if it looks really cluttered, it draws the eye to the cave underneath, and the room will look even *more* cluttered than it really is. A bed skirt can help hide this storage area. Whittle down your items to the ones that need to be in your bedroom or to the items that are used often. For everything else, use the garage, the attic, or a spare closet. Even better—sell it, donate it, or toss it.

Clean the Room

Clean the corners of your room, and dust the fans and lamps with a microfiber cloth. Wipe off all surfaces and baseboards from highest to lowest with all-purpose cleaner. Vacuum or sweep and mop the floors, taking care to move the furniture and get underneath.

 future project

Be creative with jewelry storage. Peg-Board and hooks on a wall work well if you have mostly costume jewelry. You can also use this option for your handbags. A picture frame with corkboard in the center works well for necklaces and bracelets; use thumbtacks as hooks. A screen from an old window is good for earrings, and it can be inserted into a picture frame. Hang these in your closet, or display them on your bedroom walls for personalized art.

Organize the Room

Invest in under-the-bed storage boxes because this area is a dust magnet. If these items are worth keeping, then you need to treat them well. From now on, store everything in containers. If you opt for the see-through, plastic type, hide them with a simple bed skirt (if you have basic sewing skills, you can easily make one with some flat sheets). Baskets and canvas bags work beautifully for storage, but don't forget the cheaper option of covering basic boxes with scrapbook paper, wrapping paper, or wallpaper.

Your bedroom is definitely a place to make your own. Keep the things that you love, and get rid of the rest. You won't miss them, I promise, and you'll end up loving what remains even more.

 reflection question

Does your bedroom reflect both you and your spouse? You're blessed if both of you have similar décor tastes, but all too often, men get short-changed on rooms that reflect their style. Collaborate together on some ideas that describe your ideal bedroom. Then pick one or two of those ideas, and see if you can incorporate them into your current space. Perhaps you could paint one focal wall a signature color or invest in some new bedding. Whatever it is, make it something on which you both agree.

Master Bedroom Checklist:

DECLUTTER

- ☐ Clothes
- ☐ Closet
- ☐ Nightstands
- ☐ Under the bed
- ☐ Dresser
- ☐ Rest of the room
- ☐ _____
- ☐ _____
- ☐ _____

CLEAN

- ☐ Closet
- ☐ Nightstands
- ☐ Under the bed
- ☐ Dresser
- ☐ Ceiling fan
- ☐ Crown molding
- ☐ Baseboards

- ☐ Doors
- ☐ Doorknobs
- ☐ Other furniture
- ☐ Rest of the room
- ☐ _____
- ☐ _____
- ☐ _____

ORGANIZE

- ☐ Clothes
- ☐ Closet
- ☐ Nightstands
- ☐ Under the bed
- ☐ Dresser
- ☐ Rest of the room
- ☐ _____
- ☐ _____
- ☐ _____
- ☐ _____

DAY 10:

15 | Entryways and Coat Closet

"We don't need to increase our goods nearly as much as we need to scale down our wants. Not wanting something is as good as possessing it."

—DONALD HORBAN

It's easy to overlook a lot of the little nooks and crannies of a home, but these spots really make a difference when we keep them clutter free and organized. Like it or not, the front porch and entryway of a home set the stage for what's inside, and it's all too easy to judge a book by its cover. Keep this area simple and fresh, and you're more apt to keep the rest of the house the same way.

The Game Plan

We're almost done with our ten days to a simpler home. The hard areas have been tackled, and today, we're focusing on the front entry, coat closet, hallway, and back entry.

What you'll need:

CLEANERS

☐ Glass cleaner*

☐ All-purpose cleaner*

☐ Baking soda

TOOLS

☐ Microfiber cloth

☐ Vacuum or broom, dustpan, and mop

☐ Newspaper

☐ Tub brush

☐ Broom for outside use

☐ Sponge

☐ Water hose

☐ Glue (optional)

☐ Welcome mat (optional)

☐ Your give and sell boxes

☐ Price tags and marker

* Homemade recipes for these cleaners are found in appendix A.

What's the Purpose of These Spaces?

You might think these areas serve only as portals to other rooms in the home. While that's true, they also serve as landing spots for lots of gear, and they set the stage for welcoming family members and guests. Do you want your home to feel inviting and hospitable? Would you like your daily essentials to have specific homes so that you no longer frantically search for things like your keys? Would you like to have an outdoor space where your family can enjoy the weather? The front and back entries serve these purposes. Write down your priorities for these places, and post them prominently for your work today. And don't forget about your family purpose statement.

Declutter the Front Entry

You may not have much stuff out in the open in your front entry, but it still needs decluttering. Sort through the coat closet, regardless of its location, and weed out the coats and jackets that no one wears. Put them in the sell or give boxes. What's on the closet floor or the top shelves? Pull everything out, and sort through it. This closet is a smart place to store things you don't need all the time, like seasonal items, but you still need room for the things that *do* belong in a coat closet.

Make sure your superfluous storage doesn't crowd out space for daily necessities like jackets, bags, cold-weather gear, and things like your cell phone, your keys, and possibly even a place to empty your wallet of receipts. If there's not enough room in this area, then make room. Store Christmas decorations and other seldom-used items somewhere else. If you have more floor space than closet space in your front entry, consider buying a furniture piece that can house daily necessities, such as keys, umbrellas, and dog leads. A simple, small dresser works well, if you have the room.

Clean the Front Entry

Dust and wipe down the closet and front entry doors and flat surfaces with a microfiber cloth. Use a broom or a long-handled duster to reach the ceiling corners to knock down cobwebs, and sweep and mop or vacuum the floor. Make sure to get the baseboards. Clean any windows with glass cleaner and newspaper.

Organize the Front Entry

Now's the time to create a landing spot for the things you grab as you head out the door. Create a specific spot for keys, wallets, bags, hats, scarves, and sunglasses. Use attractive containers you're happy to dis play. When you have an official designated spot for specific things, you'll habitually store them there every time, which means fewer mad hunts for things as you rush out the door.

Make Your Space Work For You

There are a variety of ideas to make this area one that works for you; there are no hard-and-fast rules for creating a uniform, perfect spot. Here are a few options for organizing your front entry:

1. **Keep it all in your coat closet.** If you're blessed to have a large enough coat closet, add simple storage shelves inside to house your

purse, your keys, your sunglasses, and your kids' backpacks. Use baskets on all the shelves, labeled with each person's name. Everyone is responsible for keeping his or her basket in order.

You might even want an additional basket just for receipts. In our family, my husband and I empty our wallets of receipts right at the front door so that I always know where all the receipts are when I update our bank accounts each week.

Use two large containers to house outdoor gear like hats, gloves, and pool toys. Divide the items seasonally, and keep the current season's box within reach, with the other container stored out of the way until it's time to switch.

2. Keep it organized and out in the open. Your coat closet might be located elsewhere, or perhaps it's so minuscule that it barely has enough room to hold one jacket per family member. In this case, use the space just past your front door. You probably don't have much floor space, so think vertically. A system of pegs on the wall can store bags, coats, and purses. Find a wall-mounted organizing system to hang your keys on and to store the day's mail.

Find a simple chest of drawers and repurpose it for this area, or even use a small bookcase with baskets. Create the same system suggested for the closet—assign one basket per person, where everyone can toss his or her stuff.

If you have an electrical outlet in the front entry, this is a great place to store charging docks for cell phones, MP3 players, and PDA devices. You can even drill a small hole in the back of one of the dresser's drawers and thread the cords through; that way, all of your gadgets can be stored inside the dresser out of sight.

future project

To spice up your front entry, paint the inside walls of your closet a contrasting color that works well with the rest of your entry space. This will add depth to the space and create an unexpected burst of color right at your front door.

3. Create a hybrid system of both ideas. If you have a closet in your front entry, you don't necessarily need to close the closet door to hide the clutter. If you're short on entryway space, try removing the closet door and transforming the closet into more of a nook. You can still use the hanging space, but add a little bench seat with storage baskets and a row of hooks on the wall. This creates a cozy spot for your catchalls, and it adds dimension to your front entry.

What About Shoes?

In most cultures worldwide, people take their shoes off before walking through the house. This is typically because in most places, people walk everywhere and don't want to track the outdoors inside. In the United States, it's common to drive everywhere, stepping foot outdoors only between the house and the car, and then between the parking lot and the final destination. So it's simply not as big a deal to wear "dirty" shoes inside.

But it is remarkable how much dirt we really do track inside when we wear our shoes in our home. Try making a spot at your front entry for people to remove their shoes. We have a simple console cabinet that we've repurposed into a shoe closet. We toss our everyday shoes inside and shut the door behind them (we keep shoes we don't typically wear daily in our bedroom closets). Then we also have a shoe rack on display so that our guests have a place to easily take off their shoes. A classic trunk or bench could serve this same purpose.

If you do choose to have a "shoes off" policy, provide inexpensive house shoes or slippers in a variety of sizes for guests to wear when it's chilly. And if they ultimately choose to wear their outdoor shoes inside, don't take it personally. Most Americans simply don't think about removing their shoes as part of a customary process of entering a home.

Declutter and Clean Outside the Front Door

Move outside to your front porch or landing. Do you have dead plants that have no hope of resurrecting? Get rid of them. Are they dying, but could possibly flourish with a little care? Retreat them to your back porch—you can tend to them later. How does your welcome mat look? If it's faded, dirty, or torn, see if a simple cleaning gives it new life. Scrub it with a tub brush and some water. If cleaning doesn't help, add a new mat to your shopping list; they're usually inexpensive, and they add new life to the front entrance.

Sweep away dead leaves, bugs, cobwebs, and miscellaneous muck on the ground. Because this really is the location where people make their first impression of your home, keep it as clear and decluttered as possible.

Clean off the front door's smudges and stains. Use your all-purpose cleaner and a sponge, or if your door is a bit on the smeary side, baking soda cuts grease well.

Repair minor wear and chips in the front door's frame with glue.

Give your porch a good bath by spraying it with a hose.

Finally, clean the most visible windows from the front entrance with glass cleaner and newspaper.

Organize Outside the Front Door

Does the outside of your home say, "Someone lives here and loves this place?" Place a simple potted plant near the door. Living plants breathe life and color into a front entry. The entrance is a fun place for seasonal décor, but don't go overboard—keep yours low maintenance. A simple wreath, a plain pumpkin in the fall, or a well-loved flowering plant is more inviting than kitschy holiday gear.

Declutter and Clean the Back Entry

Like a master bedroom, the area just outside the back door tends to get neglected; it's the last place people keep neat. In fact, home dwellers can often be so tired of cleaning the inside that when it's time to focus on the backyard, they accomplish the bare essentials.

I know you're probably ready for a break, but stick with the plan for just a few more minutes, and tackle your back porch or balcony. Perform the same procedure as you did for the front porch—sweep away leaves, bugs, and dirt, and get rid of any clutter. If you've got plants teetering on their last breath, or if you moved your front entry plants back here, put them in one spot, and create a makeshift gardening station.

Clean off the doormat, and clean off the door itself with your all-purpose cleaner. Then hose off the area with water, and use a scrub brush if needed.

Organize the Back Entry

Keep like things together. Store all of your barbecue gear in the same area, house your soil and potting tools in one location, and gather outdoor toys into one place. If you don't have a garage, use large, waterproof containers with lids. Give each category its own container when possible.

If you have room, make plans to create a sitting or dining area outside your back door. It's important to your family's health to regularlly spend time outside, and a simple landing spot for relaxation makes this more possible. A simple picnic table and benches are great for outdoor meals, and chairs and console tables found at yard sales can create an eclectic, comfortable sitting area for reading or talking.

Bonus Task

You've had a busy ten days, and I hope everyone in the family has contributed elbow grease. Your final task? Go out to eat. Have a picnic in the park, go to your favorite restaurant, or simply barbecue in your backyard. Relish in your newly improved home. It has just been transformed into a home that reflects a simpler life—a life that your family can embrace.

reflection question

Pretend like you're walking into your home for the first time. What's the general feel of your place? The front entry is one of the best places to make your home inviting and friendly. Create some simple, homemade wall art or display family photos to set the stage for the rest of your home.

Entryway Checklist:

DECLUTTER
- ☐ Entryway
- ☐ Coat closet
- ☐ Front porch
- ☐ Back entry

CLEAN
- ☐ Entryway
- ☐ Coat closet

- ☐ Front porch
- ☐ Windows
- ☐ Back entry

ORGANIZE
- ☐ Coat closet
- ☐ Laundry spot
- ☐ Front porch
- ☐ Back entry

16 | Simple Living

A Journey, Not a Destination

"Fear less, hope more; eat less, chew more; whine less, breathe more; talk less, say more; love more, and all good things will be yours."

−SWEDISH PROVERB

Recall the definition of simple living given earlier in this book—*living holistically with your life's purpose. Live* is a verb, and *living holistically* implies an ongoing, present-tense action. To live is to dwell, to be aware, to breathe in and out.

You cannot check off "live life" on a to-do list. It's an ongoing task until our last second on earth. We wake up, continue living, go to sleep, inhale and exhale while we rest, and then wake up and start anew the next morning.

So, too, does *simple* living. The process doesn't stop. The time will never arrive when you have created a simple life once and for all. We can (and should) create reachable goals that point us in the direction of simplifying our life, but at the end of the day, the stake in the path that marks our crossing that goal leads only to the next goal. We are creatures that relish in plans, in milestones, and in accomplishments. When we check something off the list, we look for the next task.

Use this to your advantage, but don't create some lofty, improbable objective of simple living that doesn't really exist. Live life in the present, and accept that simple living is a *process*, a journey.

It's a noble pursuit for the rest of your life. Enjoy the process of collecting less stuff, amassing more wisdom, having more time to relish in the little things, and coveting very little.

Simple living is also a family affair. An active and passionate pursuit of simplifying life, especially at home, works best and generates the most success when every family member is on board. If someone in your clan reluctantly agrees to help organize, sort, and clean but isn't emotionally on board, there will be tension. Family unity is absolutely essential when it comes to creating a simple home.

This is why the family purpose statement is so vital, but even that statement will just be words on paper if not every adult in the family agrees with what's written. Don't pursue the *idea* of simple living at the cost of your precious relationships. What a loss it would be to push a lofty agenda of simplicity so much that you lose the intimacy and connection of the family members you love most. Remember, relationships are more important than things. You could also say that relationships are more important than the concept of simple living.

There are also many ways to live simply. This book is meant to serve as your road map to getting off on the right foot, but it's not your complete GPS. By that, I mean that there are plenty of ideas here to get you going, but they're only the tip of the iceberg—you've got your whole life to carve out what it means for *you* to live simply. There are many avenues, paths, and directions to take once you've made the commitment to simplify your life, so be on the lookout for ways to still be uniquely you (and unique as a family) while embracing the idea that life doesn't have to be complicated.

If you truly feel inspired to simplify your life, don't give up, but also don't be a self-inflicted martyr. Show unenthusiastic family members some grace. Simplify those things you can without trampling on the hesitant. Watching you live out simplicity may be all the convincing your family member needs to be inspired to pursue passionate simplicity in every area of your family's life.

In this ongoing process of simplifying your life, don't get discouraged. You will probably take two steps forward and one step back—quite a few times. I will, too. As you tackle your home using the ten-day process described in part two of this book, there's a chance you might lose steam and move on to something else. Don't let these minor setbacks cause you to reach for the credit cards and fill a shopping cart with more stuff. You're not a failure at simple living. You're human.

Don't give up. Refer to your family purpose statement, vocalize your frustrations to a friend, and seek camaraderie with someone who shares your conviction about simple living. Give yourself some grace. Remember, it's a journey. Living holistically with your life's purpose isn't easy. It's simple, but it isn't easy.

In the end, you're golden when you just start *somewhere*. It doesn't really matter how far you still have to go toward simplifying your life, so long as you're moving forward. Remember writer Elisabeth Elliot's wise words, "When you don't know what to do, do the thing in front of you." If you feel stuck, just do *something*. Anything. Throw out the trash, clean out the fridge, or organize a bookshelf. See? You're one step closer.

I truly hope this book serves as a motivator, as a springboard, and as practical inspiration in this season of your family's life. May your life be filled with only the necessary and the beautiful.

Recipes

Making your own cleaning supplies and toiletries is cheaper, healthier, and better for the environment. As a parent, I like that I can clean while my children are awake without worry. And because skin is our largest and most porous organ, it only makes sense to not lather on the chemicals if you have a natural alternative.

Try these recipes as you run out of your store-bought cleaners and toiletries, and see if you don't get hooked.

A Note About Essential Oils

Essential oils are liquids distilled (usually by steam or water) from the leaves, stems, flowers, bark, roots, or other elements of plants. Each oil contains the true essence of the plant it was derived from. They are highly concentrated, and a little goes a long way.

Using essential oils is optional in any of these recipes, but I recommend giving them a try. They smell great, are completely natural substances, remove toxic mold and stale air, and kill viruses, bacteria, and dust mites. For cleaning, my favorite essential oils are lavender, orange, lemon, grapefruit, and tea tree (which is one of the best natural antiseptics in existence). Find these oils at health food stores or online.

Homemade Cleaning Recipes

Always test a small, inconspicuous area before cleaning an entire surface with any of these recipes. Floors and wooden surfaces may have finishes that can be harmed. The dye in carpet and upholstery may not be colorfast.

What You'll Need:

- ☐ Baking soda
- ☐ Borax
- ☐ Hydrogen peroxide
- ☐ Lemons or lemon juice
- ☐ Olive oil
- ☐ Salt—any type is fine
- ☐ Unscented soap—it can be in liquid, powder, flake, or bar form (Ivory is a common brand)

- ☐ Washing soda
- ☐ White vinegar
- ☐ Essential oils (optional)
- ☐ A few empty and cleaned spray bottles (You can reuse commercial cleaner bottles if they are cleaned well to remove remaining chemicals.)
- ☐ A few medium-sized containers with lids

All-Purpose Cleaner

¼ cup white vinegar

2 tbsp. baking soda

¼ gallon (1 liter) hot water

A few drops of essential oil (optional)

Combine the ingredients in a bucket, stir, and let the mixture cool for a few minutes before pouring it into a spray bottle.

Carpet and Upholstery Cleaner

Equal parts white vinegar and water

A few drops of essential oil (optional)

Combine the ingredients in a spray bottle and shake.

Carpet Cleaner, Heavy-Duty

Equal parts salt, white vinegar, and borax

Mix the ingredients into a paste, rub on the affected area, and let it sit for a few hours. Then scrub away with a brush or damp cloth. Make only what you need each time because it doesn't store well.

Dishwasher Soap

Equal parts borax and washing soda

Mix the ingredients and store in a labeled container. Use the amount normally called for in your dishwasher. If your water is hard, you might want to increase the proportion of washing soda.

Furniture Polish

¼ cup olive oil

4 tbsp. white vinegar

2 tbsp. lemon juice

Combine the ingredients in a spray bottle, and shake well before use. If you make extra, store it in the refrigerator because the lemon juice will sour. Please note: This cleaner should only be used on unvarnished wood furniture. See chapter 10 for more information.

Glass Cleaner

2 tsp. white vinegar

¼ gallon (1 liter) water

A few drops of essential oil (lemon cuts grease well)

Combine the ingredients in a spray bottle and shake. Works best by wiping the surface with crumpled newspaper.

Laundry Soap

> 1 cup unscented, dye-free soap (such as Ivory), grated or ground
> with a food processor
>
> ½ cup washing soda
>
> ½ cup borax
>
> A few drops of essential oil for scent (optional)

Combine the ingredients and store in a labeled container. Use 1 table-spoon for lighter loads; 2 tablespoons for heavy loads.

Mold Remover

> 1 part hydrogen peroxide
>
> 2 parts water
>
> A few drops of tea tree essential oil (optional)

Mix the ingredients in a spray bottle. Let the cleaner sit on the stain for about an hour before scrubbing off.

Oven Cleaner

> ¾ cup baking soda
>
> ¼ cup salt
>
> ¼ cup water

Mix ingredients into a paste and spread the paste over a dampened area. Let it sit overnight, and then scrape it off and rinse clean.

Toilet Bowl Cleaner

> ¼ cup baking soda
>
> 1 cup white vinegar

Combine the ingredients and pour into the toilet. Let it sit for a few min-utes, and then scrub with a toilet brush and rinse.

What You'll Need:

- ☐ Baking soda
- ☐ Apple cider vinegar (with the mother, if possible)
- ☐ Castor oil
- ☐ Extra virgin olive oil, jojoba oil, grapeseed oil, or flax-seed oil
- ☐ Coconut oil
- ☐ Stevia
- ☐ Peppermint extract (optional)
- ☐ Essential oils (optional)
- ☐ Cornstarch
- ☐ Empty squeeze bottles (or empty shampoo bottles)
- ☐ Small lidded jar or squeeze tube
- ☐ Empty deodorant container

Homemade Toiletry Recipes

These recipes are mild and use natural ingredients, so they should be safe for most skin and hair types. If you experience any irritation using these recipes, stop using them and consult your doctor.

Hair Cleanser

This is a natural replacement for shampoo.

> 1 tbsp. baking soda
>
> 1 cup water

Combine the ingredients in a squirt bottle and shake. To use, thoroughly douse your hair with water, then squeeze the mixture directly onto your hair, starting at the crown. Use your fingertips to scrub your scalp for a few minutes. Rinse out the mixture, and follow with hair clarifier.

There may be a "waiting period" when your hair feels oily. It should pass. If it continues to feel oily after six weeks, try increasing the pro- portion of baking soda. If your hair feels dry or straw-like, decrease the amount of baking soda. Also, you don't need to use this hair cleanser as often as you use shampoo because you aren't stripping your scalp's natural oils. One to three times per week should do the trick. For more information, head to SimpleMom.net and search "shampoo-free."

Hair Clarifier

This is a natural replacement for conditioner.

1 tbsp. apple cider vinegar

1 cup water

Combine the ingredients in a squirt bottle and shake. To use, thoroughly rinse out the hair cleanser and then squeeze a very small amount of hair clarifier onto the ends of your hair (take care to avoid your scalp). Let it rest on your hair for a few seconds, and then rinse.

The healthiest apple cider vinegar still has the "mother," which is the bulk concentration of enzymes— –it will make the vinegar look cloudy or stringy. If you use apple cider vinegar with the mother, simply shake your hair clarifier before using to evenly distribute the enzymes. If your hair still feels too dry, try replacing the vinegar with honey.

"Oil Cleansing Method" Facial Cleanser

Castor oil

Extra-virgin olive oil (EVOO), jojoba oil, grapeseed oil, or flaxseed oil

Combine the ingredients in a small bottle and shake. This is a natural replacement for facial cleanser. Contrary to popular belief, oil does not cause oily skin or acne. That culprit is usually a combination of hormones, trapped bacteria, and dirt. Like your hair, the sebum that the skin secretes is actually good for your skin—it protects it from the outside environment and keeps harmful things from seeping in.

The ratio of oils depends mostly on your skin type. Start with these ratios, and experiment with what works best for you:

- For normal skin, you could start off with a 1-to-1 ratio of castor oil and EVOO.
- For acne-prone or oily skin, reduce the proportion of EVOO, and try 3 parts castor oil to 1 part EVOO.
- For drier skin, start off with 1 part castor oil to 3 parts EVOO.

Pour a quarter-sized amount into your palm, rub your hands together, and slowly massage your skin with your fingertips. Don't splash your face with water first—apply it dry. Don't scrub—just rub.

Next, wet a washcloth with hot water (but not scalding!), and put it over your face. Leave it in place until the cloth cools to about room temperature. Remove the washcloth, rinse and wring it, and then gently wipe off the oil.

You probably won't need to use this facial cleanser more than once per day. I prefer to use this at night, just before bed. In the morning, I simply splash my face with cold water. This cleanser also removes all makeup. For more information, head to SimpleMom.net and search *oil cleansing method*.

Basic Homemade Toothpaste

   2 tbsp. of coconut oil
   2 to 3 tbsp. of baking soda
   ¼ tsp. of Stevia powder
   A few drops of pure peppermint extract or essential oils such as lemon, clove, lime, cinnamon, peppermint, eucalyptus, or licorice (Not all essential oils are safe to ingest internally, but these are fine.)

Mix all ingredients together until the combination resembles toothpaste. Store it at room temperature in a small lidded jar, and use a small teaspoon to scoop out a small bit onto your toothbrush. Or, store it in an empty squeeze tube, which can be found in the camping section of most sporting goods stores.

Coconut oil has a melting point of 76°F (24°C), which means that this toothpaste feels more liquidy during warmer weather. It doesn't change its effectiveness, though.

Stevia provides a bit of natural sweetness, making the toothpaste palatable, as does the pure peppermint extract or the essential oils. You could try a variety of flavors.

Homemade Deodorant

¼ cup baking soda

¼ cup cornstarch

4 to 6 tbsp. coconut oil

Essential oil (optional)

Empty deodorant container

Mix the baking soda and cornstarch in a small bowl. Add the coconut oil, a tablespoon or so at a time, until all the dry ingredients have been mixed in. If you'd like a scent, add a few drops of an essential oil.

Pack the deodorant into a clean, empty deodorant container by twisting down the inside and filling it with your new deodorant. Shape it into a curve with a spoon, and apply as usual.

Make sure your coconut oil is in its solid form. It has a 76°F (24°C) melting point, so you may need to refrigerate it first for a short time if it's warmer than 76°F (24°C) in your house.

For more information, head to SimpleMom.net and search *home-made deodorant*.

Inventory Templates

In chapters 9–14, I often recommend taking inventory of certain supplies—food, clothing, and the like. In this appendix, you'll find two templates that can be used for a variety of inventory worksheets mentioned in part two. Use the closet inventory list for your clothing closets, linen closet, and coat closets. Use the food inventory list for your freezer, refrigerator, and pantry, creating a separate list for each storage area. Feel free to photocopy and enlarge each worksheet to a size that works well for your home management notebook.

Closet Inventory

Contents of _____

Item	Size	Qty	Notes
☐ _____	___	___	_____
☐ _____	___	___	_____
☐ _____	___	___	_____
☐ _____	___	___	_____
☐ _____	___	___	_____
☐ _____	___	___	_____
☐ _____	___	___	_____
☐ _____	___	___	_____
☐ _____	___	___	_____
☐ _____	___	___	_____
☐ _____	___	___	_____
☐ _____	___	___	_____
☐ _____	___	___	_____
☐ _____	___	___	_____
☐ _____	___	___	_____
☐ _____	___	___	_____
☐ _____	___	___	_____
☐ _____	___	___	_____
☐ _____	___	___	_____
☐ _____	___	___	_____

Food Inventory

Contents of _____

Food	Qty	Storage Date	Use by
☐ _____	____	_____	_____
☐ _____	____	_____	_____
☐ _____	____	_____	_____
☐ _____	____	_____	_____
☐ _____	____	_____	_____
☐ _____	____	_____	_____
☐ _____	____	_____	_____
☐ _____	____	_____	_____
☐ _____	____	_____	_____
☐ _____	____	_____	_____
☐ _____	____	_____	_____
☐ _____	____	_____	_____
☐ _____	____	_____	_____
☐ _____	____	_____	_____
☐ _____	____	_____	_____
☐ _____	____	_____	_____
☐ _____	____	_____	_____
☐ _____	____	_____	_____
☐ _____	____	_____	_____
☐ _____	____	_____	_____

Home Management Notebook Templates

There's no right or wrong way to create a home management notebook, but you might appreciate a little guidance to spark some ideas. In this appendix, you'll find templates for a variety of worksheets mentioned in this book. Feel free to photocopy and enlarge each worksheet to a size that works well for your home management notebook.

You can also download a template of each of these, plus other templates, at SimpleMom.net, on the downloads page.

1. Daily Docket
2. Daily Docket Example
3. Pocket Docket (a smaller version of the Daily Docket)
4. Cleaning Checklist
5. Weekly Schedule Worksheet
6. Weekly Schedule Worksheet Example
7. Monthly Zero-Based Budget Worksheet
8. Babysitter's Guide
9. Dual Income Worksheet

Daily Docket

Date: _____

Today's MITs:

1. _____
2. _____
3. _____

Inspiration:

What's for dinner?

(notes)

Work:

☐ _____
_____

☐ _____
_____

☐ _____
_____

☐ _____
_____

Water: ☐☐☐☐☐☐☐
Food log: ☐   Workout:

Today's to-do list:

☐ _____
☐ _____
☐ _____
☐ _____
☐ _____
☐ _____
☐ _____
☐ _____
☐ _____
☐ _____

Miscellaneous notes:

Today's general plan:

☐ _____ : _____
☐ _____ : _____
☐ _____ : _____
☐ _____ : _____
☐ _____ : _____
☐ _____ : _____
☐ _____ : _____
☐ _____ : _____
☐ _____ : _____
☐ _____ : _____
☐ _____ : _____
☐ _____ : _____
☐ _____ : _____
☐ _____ : _____
☐ _____ : _____

Daily Docket Example

Date: __July 14__

Today's MITs:

1. pay water bill
2. post office
3. return phone calls

Inspiration:

"You don't choose your family. They are God's gift to you, as you are to them." —Desmond Tutu

What's for dinner?

enchiladas, beans & rice

(notes) beans in the slow cooker
by noon

Work:

- ☐ e-mail prospective clients
- ☐ browse Internet for fabric swatches
- ☐ finish inspiration board for Mrs. Fletcher
- ☐

Water: ☐☐☐☐☐☐☐☐
Food log: ☐   Workout: family walk
after dinner

Today's to-do list:

- ☐ pay water bill
- ☐ get mom's b-day gift to post office
- ☐ return calls
- ☐ find sitter for next week's date night
- ☐ take Jane to ballet class
- ☐ organize front closet
- ☐ call Ellen about PTA meeting
- ☐ balance the checkbook
- ☐ playdate & coffee @ the Browns'
- ☐ work

Miscellaneous notes:

laundry, order soapnuts soon
PTA meeting:
settle on bake sale date

Today's general plan:

- ☐ 10am : head to Browns' for play
- ☐ _____ : date & coffee
- ☐ _____ : post office on the
- ☐ _____ : way home
- ☐ 2pm : Jane's nap
- ☐ _____ : make enchiladas & rice
- ☐ _____ : return calls
- ☐ _____ : call Ellen
- ☐ _____ : pay bills
- ☐ _____ : balance checkbook
- ☐ _____ : work
- ☐ 5-5:30 : Jane's ballet class
- ☐ _____ : Mark home from work
- ☐ _____ : enchiladas in oven
- ☐ 6pm : dinner

Pocket Docket

Date: _____

What's for dinner?_____

Today's To-Do List   MIT•

☐ _____ ☐

☐ _____ ☐

☐ _____ ☐

☐ _____ ☐

☐ _____ ☐

☐ _____ ☐

☐ _____ ☐

☐ _____ ☐

☐ _____ ☐

☐ _____ ☐

*An MIT is a Most Important Thing. You really shouldn't have more than three a day for sanity's sake.

Schedule and/or appointments

☐ _____ : _____

☐ _____ : _____

☐ _____ : _____

☐ _____ : _____

☐ _____ : _____

☐ _____ : _____

Notes:

Cleaning Checklist

DAILY
- [ ] Make beds
- [ ] Dishes
- [ ] Kitchen counters
- [ ] Pick up clutter
- [ ] Quick sweep living/ dining room
- [ ] Quick sweep kitchen
- [ ] File paperwork

WEEKLY

Living room
- [ ] Floor
- [ ] Windows
- [ ] Dust surfaces
- [ ] Declutter
- [ ] Rug

Kitchen
- [ ] Floor
- [ ] Cabinets
- [ ] Windows & balcony door
- [ ] Clean out fridge & freezer

Main bathroom
- [ ] Countertop
- [ ] Toilet
- [ ] Tub
- [ ] Mirror
- [ ] Soap refill
- [ ] Floor

Master bathroom
- [ ] Countertop
- [ ] Toilet
- [ ] Shower
- [ ] Mirror
- [ ] Soap refill
- [ ] Floor

Guest bedroom
- [ ] Floor
- [ ] Windows
- [ ] Dust surfaces
- [ ] Declutter

Kids' bedrooms
- [ ] Floor
- [ ] Windows
- [ ] Dust surfaces
- [ ] Declutter

Master bedroom
- [ ] Floor
- [ ] Windows
- [ ] Dust surfaces
- [ ] Declutter

Front entry & hall
- [ ] Floor
- [ ] Dust surfaces
- [ ] Declutter
- [ ] Rugs

Balcony/backyard
- [ ] Clean surfaces
- [ ] Declutter
- [ ] Tend to garden

Laundry
- [ ] Bedding
- [ ] Towels
- [ ] Clothing

Finances
- [ ] Balance accounts
- [ ] Pay bills
- [ ] Inventory cash
- [ ] Update monthly budget
- [ ] Update work expense report

Food
- [ ] Grocery shopping
- [ ] Market shopping
- [ ] Prep & make-ahead cooking

Miscellaneous
- [ ] _____
- [ ] _____

MONTHLY TASKS
- [ ] Organize pantry
- [ ] Food inventory
- [ ] Menu plan
- [ ] Write budget
- [ ] Organize bathroom stuff
- [ ] Organize wardrobes

Weekly Schedule Worksheet

Day of week: _____

6 AM	_____	_____	_____
7:00	_____	_____	_____
8:00	_____	_____	_____
9:00	_____	_____	_____
10:00	_____	_____	_____
11:00	_____	_____	_____
12 PM	_____	_____	_____
1:00	_____	_____	_____
2:00	_____	_____	_____
3:00	_____	_____	_____
4:00	_____	_____	_____
5:00	_____	_____	_____
6:00	_____	_____	_____
7:00	_____	_____	_____
8:00	_____	_____	_____
9:00	_____	_____	_____
10:00	_____	_____	_____
11:00	_____	_____	_____
12 AM	_____	_____	_____

Weekly Schedule Worksheet Example

Day of week: __Monday__

	Mom	Dad	Jane
6 AM	exercise		
7:00	laundry		
8:00	breakfast	breakfast	breakfast
9:00	clean	work	play
10:00	↓		
11:00	read to Jane		
12 PM	↓		↓
1:00	lunch		lunch
2:00	work		nap
3:00			↓
4:00	↓		play
5:00	make dinner	↓	↓
6:00	dinner	dinner	dinner
7:00			bath
8:00	bills/budget	movie/TV	bed
9:00			
10:00			
11:00	bed	bed	
12 AM			

Monthly Zero-Based Budget Worksheet

INCOME

Income 1_____

Income 2 _____

Other _____

Other _____

Other _____

Other _____

Other _____

Total Income _____

EXPENSES

Charitable

Giving _____

Other _____

Savings

Emergency fund _____

College fund _____

Retirement fund _____

Housing

First mortgage _____

Second mortgage _____

Rent _____

Taxes _____

Insurance _____

Repairs* _____

Furniture replacement*_____

Other _____

Utilities

Electricity _____

Water/trash _____

Gas _____

Phone _____

Cell phone _____

Cable_____

Food

Groceries_____

Transportation

Gas & oil_____

Repairs & tires _____

Vehicle insurance*_____

License & taxes* _____

Car replacement* _____

Clothing

Children* _____

Adults*_____

Cleaning/laundry_____

Month/Year: _____

Medical

Disability insurance _____

Health insurance _____

Life insurance _____

Doctor* _____

Dentist* _____

Optometrist* _____

Medications* _____

Personal

Toiletries/cosmetics* _____

Hair care* _____

School tuition* _____

School supplies* _____

Child support _____

Alimony _____

Gifts & holidays* _____

Other _____

Fun

Entertainment _____

Restaurants _____

Vacation* _____

Debt

Bank loan _____

Credit card _____

Credit card _____

School loan _____

School loan _____

Car payment _____

Car payment _____

Other _____

Other _____

Total Expenses _____

Income _____

Minus Expenses _____

Total _____

(this should be zero)

* These are sinking funds. That means you set aside an amount each month for a category, whether or not you spend it this month. To calculate how much you should save, total the amount you'll need this year and then divide by twelve.

Babysitter's Guide

Copy a set of these guides and use a new one each time, or print one, write down the permanent information, and keep it in a clear sleeve. Then use a dry-erase marker to write down the temporary info.

Where we'll be: _____

When we'll return: _____

Parents' name & cell phones:

_____ #_____

_____ #_____

Home address & phone number

_____

_____

General family rules (TV, movies, play, foods allowed, etc.):

_____

In an emergency...

Emergency name, number, & relationship:

_____

_____

Emergency name, number, & relationship:

_____

_____

Poison Control: _____

Medical insurance info: _____

_____

Other: _____

In a serious emergency, please call 911 first and then call us.

Children

Name & age: _____

Favorites: _____

_____

Allergies: _____

Medications:_____

Bedtime: _____

Additional rules:_____

Name & age: _____

Favorites: _____

_____

Allergies: _____

Medications:_____

Bedtime: _____

Additional rules:_____

Name & age: _____

Favorites: _____

_____

Allergies: _____

Medications:_____

Bedtime: _____

Additional rules:_____

Name & age: _____

Favorites: _____

_____

Allergies: _____

Medications:_____

Bedtime: _____

Additional rules:_____

Dual Income Worksheet

Should both adults work? This is a difficult modern-day question that doesn't always have a clear answer. When both adults in the family work, you net more money. But there are a number of expenses associated with working outside the home, and they can really add up. Use this simple worksheet to do the math for your family. Is it financially reasonable for both adults to work outside the home? Then think over some questions about quality of life. This worksheet won't give you a clear answer, but it will be a springboard to aid in discussing this issue.

Additional Paycheck Information

Net monthly pay: _____

Total monthly expenses: _____

Pay minus expenses: _____

Additional Monthly Expenses Because of Working

Child care: _____

Food: _____

Transportation: _____

Cleaning & home maintenance services:

_____

Other

_____ $_____

_____ $_____

_____ $_____

Questions Regarding the Additional Paycheck

1. How important are the careers to both spouses?
2. How important is advancement in these careers?
3. Is it possible for one (or both) spouses to work from home?
4. What are some household tasks that can be done if one spouse doesn't work (such as coupon clipping)?
5. How will this decision affect the children's education?
6. What are additional positives to both spouses working outside the home?
7. What are additional negatives to both spouses working outside the home?

Choices for a Simpler Life

Life is full of choices. When you approach simple living, sometimes the decision is clear-cut. Sometimes it's not. Here are some everyday choices you might face, along with some questions to spark your brain and help you make a wise decision.

1. Should I tend my own garden or shop at my local farmers' market?

Pros to tending your own garden:

- You have freedom in choosing what to harvest.
- It's cost-effective. The price of supplies required is typically lower than the value of the food output.
- It's a family activity that teaches botany, the origins of your food, and a good work ethic, all while promoting family unity.
- The physical labor required promotes exercise, a good work ethic, and an appreciation of nature, which will benefit you and your family members.

Pros to shopping at your local farmers' market:

- It takes less time and energy than planting, tending, and harvesting your own garden.
- Shopping at a farmers' market supports the local economy.
- Shopping at a farmers' market is a family activity that teaches community, farming, respect for food, and supporting small and local businesses.
- You probably have more variety and choices in produce.

My thoughts: It's entirely possible to enjoy both of these options. There are so many benefits to both cultivating a plot of your own land *and* to shopping at a community farmers' market that it's hard to argue for not doing either.

In our family, we grow a very small amount of herbs and veggies in containers on our balcony. The rest of our produce comes from our local farmers' market. Check the resources section at the end of the book for finding a local farmers' market near you. You'll also find resources for gardening tips.

2. Should I take the time to clip coupons?

Pros to clipping coupons:

- It can provide substantial savings on items you would buy anyway.
- Stockpiling is easier because you can buy large amounts to save for later at a discounted price.
- It helps you be more selective while shopping.
- Involving your children teaches them the basics of home economics, saving, and money management.

Cons to clipping coupons:

- It's time-consuming.
- It might tempt you to buy more than you need.
- Without an organized system, it can add to the clutter at home.

My thoughts: Coupon clipping can be a major contribution to the family budget, especially if you have the time to do it well. There is a method to effectively clipping coupons, however, so it's important to do so strategically and wisely. If you clip everything in sight, you'll add to the clutter, require more organization, and be tempted to buy items you wouldn't normally purchase. Check the resources section for Web sites that teach you how to use coupons to your advantage.

3. Should I line-dry my laundry or use my clothes dryer?

Pros to line-drying:

- It's cost-effective, saving you money on your electric bill.
- It uses natural power (sun and wind), making it eco-friendly.
- Clothes last longer when they're line-dried.
- It often eliminates the need for a commercial stain remover, because sunlight is a great natural stain remover.

- Involving your children in hanging the laundry teaches them the value of caring of your family's possessions as well as community effort, and the natural world and its benefits. It also inspires a strong work ethic.

Pros to using your clothes dryer:

- Clothes will dry faster in the colder months.
- It's less time-consuming.
- It requires less space, particularly if you don't have a backyard or a large balcony.
- Sometimes line drying isn't allowed in certain neighborhoods, making a dryer your only choice.

My thoughts: Our family does both. In the late spring and summer months, we almost exclusively line-dry. Clothes dry surprisingly fast, and we enjoy spending time together and talking as we hang the laundry. It also offsets some of the cost of air conditioning during the summer months. We use our dryer more often during the wet winter months, though we still line-dry cloth diapers and a few quick-to-dry items. I typically hang a load of laundry to dry indoors overnight, and it's ready by morning.

4. Should we have a landline phone in addition to cell phones, or cell phones only?

Pros to having a landline:

- People without a cell phone will have access to a phone while at your home.
- No need to worry about getting good reception inside your house.
- It makes it possible to have dial-up Internet access.

Pros to having only a cell phone:

- It's cheaper—there's no landline phone bill. With the right cell phone plan, you won't pay extra for minutes or services.
- Depending on your cell phone plan, you have free (or much cheaper) long-distance service.
- Depending on your cell phone plan, calling can be free within your household.
- More and more people are relying solely on cell phones, anyway. Your landline might not be used often enough to justify its cost.

My thoughts: When we live in the United States, we use only cell phones. We don't miss our landline a bit, and because we share a family plan, calls between my husband and me are free. Much of our extended family also uses the same cell phone provider, so we enjoy free long distance with them. When our kids are older (and therefore aren't around us quite as much), we may consider getting a landline. But we can also just as easily put them on our family's cell phone plan.

5. Should we have cable television?

Pros to having cable:

- More television choices mean more choices for entertainment.
- More television choices *might* mean more educational choices for your children.
- It makes it possible to have cable Internet access.

Cons to having cable:

- It's a nonessential bill, costing you more money.
- You'll probably be tempted to spend more time watching television.

- You'll have less control over the graphic images and just plain twaddle that enters your home.

My thoughts: Our family has never paid for cable television. This doesn't mean we don't enjoy the occasional show found exclusively on cable, but the only time cable has been in our home is when it was a free benefit in a rental apartment. And when we had it, we definitely watched more television than we originally intended. We haven't had any television access in three years, and we don't miss it. We still have a TV for movies, and we can follow the news on the Internet. And with services like Hulu.com, we can watch most any television show online. There's a chance we may get cable in the future, but for us, it's definitely a luxury, not a necessity.

6. Should we use cloth or disposable diapers?

Pros to using cloth diapers:
- The one-time cost of purchasing cloth diapers is less than the cost of continually buying disposable diapers.
- Your baby's skin won't touch toxins such as toluene, ethylbenzene, xylene, dipentene, dioxin, and chlorine (which are commonly found in disposable diapers).
- You are contributing less trash to the landfills.
- Your child may potty train faster. Studies have shown that babies wearing cloth are aware of a wet diaper at a younger age.

Pros to using disposable diapers:
- They don't require a large one-time cost up front.
- You have a little less laundry.
- They take a little less time.

My thoughts: Our family switched to cloth diapers when my second-born was a year old, and we haven't looked back. It has saved us so much money, and it is much faster and easier to wash and dry them than I initially thought. We still use the occasional disposable diaper for long travel, but cloth remains our default.

7. Should we become a one-car family?

Pros to having only one car:

- You can use the money you would have spent on a car to purchase something else.
- You'll have fewer ongoing costs from things such as gasoline, repairs, maintenance, licenses, and taxes.
- You'll spend more time as a family because it's more difficult to go your separate ways.
- You'll be more intentional in your time management because you'll have to coordinate using the car as a family.
- You'll contribute less pollution and less fossil fuel consumption to the environment.
- You may get more exercise because you might rely more on a bicycle or your own two feet.

Cons to having only one car:

- You're not as free and independent to travel.
- It might limit your choices of employment, entertainment, and community involvement.

My thoughts: In most cultures around the world, families only have one car, if they have one at all. Having two or more vehicles in one household is truly an American phenomenon, but it's what Americans consider normal. I live overseas with my family, and we have only one car—and for several years, we relied solely on public transportation. I admit that having a vehicle is a much-appreciated luxury with small children, but we certainly don't have a need for more than one. My husband often walks to work, and if he needs the car, we arrange our family plans so that I stay home that day.

8. Should we buy groceries in bulk and shop less often, or buy smaller amounts and shop more often?

Pros to buying in bulk:

- You might save money to buy a larger quantity.
- It may eliminate the need for future errands.
- You'll have plenty of staple items when you need them.

Cons to buying in bulk:

- You might spend more money by buying more than you need.
- Buying in bulk requires the space to store the larger quantities.
- If you buy in bulk at a warehouse-type store, you may *still* need to go to a traditional grocery store.

My thoughts: I think the ultimate "best" choice depends on the size of your family and the type of food you prefer. Bulk warehouses can provide good deals for boxed goods and nonperishables, but if you rely mostly on fresh produce, it's not quite as good a deal. However, if you have a large family and consume bulk-sized items in a reasonable amount of time, bulk shopping can be an affordable choice. We occasionally buy staples at warehouses—vitamins, snacks, and the like, but for everyday shopping, we stick to the farmers' market and the neighborhood grocery store.

9. This year, should we take one large family vacation or have a few weekend getaways?

Pros to taking one large vacation:

- You'll have a chance to go somewhere different and farther away.
- You'll only have to pack—and unpack—for one vacation.
- You may save money by staying in a hotel only once a year.
- You may have a chance to more fully relax.

Pros to taking a few weekend getaways:

- You can explore your local environment.
- You may save money by traveling a shorter distance (such as driving instead of flying).
- You'll have a wider variety of vacation types—more kid-friendly one weekend, more adventurous the next, for example.

My thoughts: Our family enjoys both of these options, typically alternating years. If we take a large family vacation one year, we'll go on a few weekend getaways the next year. Both have their merits, both can be exhausting, and both create lasting memories. It truly depends on your current financial status, your children's needs, and what your family enjoys.

Resources

Financial Health

Consumer Reports, www.consumerreports.org. Research all sorts of information about household products, vehicles, and even compare online bank options.

Dave Ramsey, www.daveramsey.com. Head to his Web site for information about his radio show, books, classes, and a database of his Endorsed Local Providers.

Deal Seeking Mom, dealseekingmom.com. A wealth of coupons, free offers, and product samples for home life.

Frugal Dad, frugaldad.com. Advice, encouragement, and personal finance stories from a father's perspective.

ING Direct, www.ingdirect.com. Consistently rated as one of the top online banks.

The Millionaire Next Door: The Surprising Secrets of America's Wealthy by Thomas J. Stanley and William D. Danko, published by Pocket.

Money Saving Mom, moneysavingmom.com. Find ideas, resources, coupon-clipping strategies, and motivation for frugal and debt-free living.

Pear Budget, www.pearbudget.com. A simple, easy-to-operate online budgeting tool that can be fully customized for your needs.

Saving for College, www.savingforcollege.com. Helpful tools to compare Coverdell Education Savings Accounts (ESAs) and 529 plans along with a list of low-cost ESAs. They also have great online calculators to help you plan.

The Total Money Makeover: A Proven Plan for Financial Fitness by Dave Ramsey, published by Thomas Nelson.

Your Money or Your Life: Transforming Your Relationship with Money and Achieving Financial Independence by Vicki Robin, Joe Dominguez and Monique Tilford, published by Penguin.

Crafting and Buying Handmade

The Creative Family: How to Encourage Imagination and Nurture Family Connections by Amanda Blake Soule, published by Trumpeter.

Etsy.com, www.etsy.com. An online marketplace of thousands of shops selling handmade goods.

Handmade Home: Simple Ways to Repurpose Old Materials Into New Family Treasures by Amanda Blake Soule, published by Trumpeter.

Lovely Design, lovelydesign.blogspot.com. Pretty tutorials and photos for crafting for and with your children.

Made by Joel, madebyjoel.blogspot.com. An inspiring crafter dad shares his tips and ideas for creative crafts.

Make and Takes, www.makeandtakes.com. Geared toward crafts for children, this site provides hundreds of ideas for kids' creativity.

Maya Made, www.mayamade.blogspot.com. Craft ideas and tutorials for both adults and children.

Soule Mama, www.soulemama.com. Full of beautiful photos, craft ideas, and inspiration to live a handmade life.

Green Living, the Outdoors, and Exploration

Backyard Homestead: Produce All the Food You Need on Just a Quarter Acre! by Carleen Madigan, published by Storey Publishing, LLC.

Free Range Kids: Giving Our Children the Freedom We Had Without Going Nuts With Worry by Lenore Skenazy, published by Jossey-Bass.

The Green Guide, www.thegreenguide.com. Tips on everything related to green living and the environment.

Green Living by E Magazine, published by Plume.

Last Child in the Woods: Saving Our Children From Nature-Deficit Disorder by Richard Louv, published by Algonquin Books.

Simple Organic, simpleorganic.net. A multi-authored blog that shares ideas, tips, and resources for greener living.

The Story of Stuff, storyofstuff.com. A compelling twenty-minute online video that visualizes the worldwide implications of having too much stuff. They have other informative online videos as well.

You Grow Girl, yougrowgirl.com. Basic tips on gardening with a helpful online community.

Food and Cooking

Animal, Vegetable, Miracle: A Year of Food Life by Barbara Kingsolver, published by HarperCollins.

The Art of Simple Food: Notes, Lessons, and Recipes From a Delicious Revolution by Alice Waters, published by Clarkson Potter.

In Defense of Food: An Eater's Manifesto by Michael Pollan, published by Penguin.

Food, Inc. distributed by Magnolia Home Entertainment. A compelling documentary about the modern-day food industry. Slightly graphic for young children.

How to Cook Everything: 2,000 Simple Recipes for Great Food by Mark Bittman, published by John Wiley & Sons, Inc.

Local Harvest, www.localharvest.org. A database of farmers' markets, community supported agriculture (CSA), and local farms.

Nourishing Traditions: The Cookbook That Challenges Politically Correct Nutrition and the Diet Dictocrats by Sally Fallon and Mary G. Enig, published by NewTrends.

Real Food Media, www.realfoodmedia.com. A network of bloggers who promote slow food, whole ingredients, and traditional cooking methods.

Simple Bites, www.simplebites.net. A collaborative site with cooking tips and recipes for families using whole foods.

Simplifying Family Life

Homemade: A Surprisingly Easy Guide to Making Hundreds of Everyday Products You Would Otherwise Buy by Reader's Digest, published by Reader's Digest.

The Power of Less: The Fine Art of Limiting Yourself to the Essential ... in Business and in Life by Leo Babauta, published by Hyperion.

Organizing Your Way, www.organizingyourway.com. Useful tips and creative ideas for organizing your home.

Seeing the Everyday, the small things magazine, www.seeingtheeveryday. com. A magazine that celebrates the ordinary things in life.

Simple Mom, simplemom.net. My Web site, where I share resources, downloads, and encouragement for keeping things simple.

Small Notebook, smallnotebook.org. Inspiration for keeping and running a simple home.

Steady Days: A Journey Toward Intentional, Professional Motherhood, by Jamie Martin, published by Infused Communications.

Steady Mom, steadymom.com. A site about nurturing deeper relationships and retaining enthusiasm in the family.

Find What You're Looking For

Amazon, www.amazon.com. The largest online store on the Internet.
Check here for the going rate of your used books, and set up a seller's
account to sell them.

Craigslist, www.craigslist.org. Free classified ads for most major cities
worldwide.

eBay, www.ebay.com. The largest online auction house on the Internet.
A good resource for checking the going rate for just about everything,
along with buying and selling.

The Freecycle Network, www.freecycle.org. A grass roots network of
people giving and getting items for free in your local community.

Half.com, www.half.ebay.com. An online marketplace for buying and
selling used goods.

IKEA, www.ikea.com. A worldwide home goods store with affordable
furniture, organizing supplies, and textiles.

Laundry Tree, www.laundrytree.com. My preferred shop for buying
soapnuts, a natural tree fruit that serves as an excellent, nontoxic
alternative to traditional laundry detergent.

Wishpot, www.wishpot.com. A free site that allows you to create wish
lists from all over the Internet, and then share them with others.

Personal Care

*Color Me Beautiful: Discover Your Natural Beauty Through the Colors
That Make You Look Great and Feel Fabulous* by Carole Jackson, published by Ballantine Books.

A Guide to Quality, Taste, & Style, by Tim Gunn, published by Abrams
Image.

Notes

1 Margot Adler, "Behind the Ever-Expanding American Dream House," NPR, http://npr. org/templates/story/story.php?storyId=5525283 (accessed August 18, 2008).

2 Alex Wilson and Jessica Boehland, "Small is Beautiful: U.S. House Size, Resource Use, and the Environment," Greener Buildings, http://www.greenerbuildings.com/ news/2005/07/12/small-beautiful-us-house-size-resource-use-and-environment (accessed August 18, 2008).

3 Demographia, "Australia & USA Have Largest Houses," http://demographia.blogspot. com/2009/01/australia-usa-have-largest-houses.html (accessed May 19, 2009).

4 Rebecca Ray and John Schmitt, "No-Vacation Nation," Center for Economic and Policy Research, http://www.cepr.net/index.php/publications/reports/no-vacation-nation/ (accessed May 19, 2009).

5 Deepa Babington, "Americans less happy today than 30 years ago: study," Reuters, http://www.reuters.com/article/idUSL1550309820070615, (accessed May 19, 2009).

6 Zachary M. Schrag, review of *The Bulldozer in the Countryside: Suburban Sprawl and the Rise of American Environmentalism*, by Adam Rome. Technology and Culture (October 2002), 802–803.

7 Randy Alcorn, *The Treasure Principle: Discovering the Secret of Joyful Giving* (Sisters, OR: Multnomah Publishers, 2001).

8 Laura Rowley, "Can You Live On One Income? It's Worth a Try," Yahoo! Finance, http://finance.yahoo.com/expert/article/moneyhappy/81176 (accessed August 29, 2009).

9 Paul Sims, "Families so busy the only time they spend together is watching TV," Daily Mail, http://www.dailymail.co.uk/news/article-1169456/Families-busy-time-spend-watching-TV.html (accessed August 27, 2009).

10 Norman Herr, "Television Statistics," The Sourcebook for Teaching Science, http://www.csun.edu/science/health/docs/tv&health.html (accessed August 27, 2009).

11 Richard Zackon, "Ground-Breaking Study of Video Viewing Finds Younger Boomers Consume More Video Media Than Any Other Group," Council for Research Excellence, http://www.researchexcellence.com/news/032609_vcm.php (accessed August 27, 2009).

12 Richard Louv, *Last Child in the Woods: Saving our Children from Nature-Deficit Disorder*. (Chapel Hill, NC: Algonquin Books of Chapel Hill, 2008).

13 Take Back Your Time, "Challenging Time Poverty," http://www.timeday.org/ (accessed May 19, 2009).

14 Deborah Lowe Vandell and Barbara Wolfe, "Child Care Quality: Does It Matter and Does it Need to be Improved?", UC Irvine Department of Education, http://www.gse.uci.edu/childcare/pdf/questionnaire_interview/Vandell%20&%20Wolfe%202000f.pdf (accessed August 27, 2009).

15 The Container Store, "Learn About Us," http://www.containerstore.com/about/index.html (accessed August 30, 2009).

16 Simply Charlotte Mason, "What is Twaddle?" http://simplycharlottemason.com/2009/09/02/what-is-twaddle/ (accessed September 15, 2009).

17 Tim Gunn, *A Guide to Quality, Taste, & Style* (New York: Abrams Image, 2007).

Index

Books of Interest

Absolutely Organize Your Family
Spend less time struggling to keep up and more time savoring everyday moments with your family. You'll find practical, effective solutions for all of your family's organizing challenges with targeted advice for your children's schedules, belongings and spaces. ISBN-13: 978-1-4403-0164-3; ISBN-10: 1-4403-0164-6, paperback, 208 pages, #Z5709

Organized Now!
Get practical, action-oriented organizing advice that you can use to organize any part of your life in less than one week. Quick, easy-to-follow checklists let you spend more time organizing and less time reading—a perfect fit for your busy lifestyle. ISBN-13: 978-1-4403-0863-5; ISBN-10: 1-4403-0863-2, hardcover with concealed spiral, 256 pages, #Z9321

No-Hassle Housecleaning
Create a healthy, clean home with less time and effort and no harsh chemicals. In-depth chapters help you quickly and effectively clean each room in your house and tackle laundry, stain removal and cleaning for pet owners. ISBN-13: 978-1-55870-881-5; ISBN-10: 1-55870-881-2, paperback, 208 pages #Z3754

These books and other fine Betterway Home titles are available at your local bookstore and from online suppliers. Visit our Web site at www.betterwaybooks.com.
